T0093786

DATA SECURITY IN CLOUD COMPUTING, VOLUME I

DATA SECURITY
IN CLOUD
COMPUTING,
VOLUME I

GIULIO D'AGOSTINO

MOMENTUM PRESS
ENGINEERING

First published in 2019 by
Momentum Press®, LLC
222 East 46th Street, New York, NY 10017
www.momentumpress.net

ISBN-13: 978-1-94708-399-8 (print)
ISBN-13: 978-1-94944-900-6 (e-book)

Momentum Press Computer Engineering Foundations, Currents, and Trajectories Collection

Cover and interior design by S4Carlisle Publishing Services Private Ltd., Chennai, India

First edition: 2019

10 9 8 7 6 5 4 3 2 1

Printed in the United States of America

Dedication

To my wife Eimear for standing beside me throughout my career and writing this book.

ABSTRACT

Cloud computing has already been adopted by many organizations and people because of its advantages of economy, reliability, scalability and guaranteed quality of service amongst others. Readers will learn specifics about software as a service (SaaS), platform as a service (PaaS), infrastructure as a service (IaaS), server and desktop virtualization, and much more.

This book covers not only information protection in cloud computing, architecture and fundamentals, but also the plan design and in-depth implementation details needed to migrate existing applications to the cloud. Readers will have a greater comprehension of cloud engineering and the actions required to rapidly reap its benefits while at the same time lowering IT implementation risk. The book's content is ideal for users wanting to migrate to the cloud, IT professionals seeking an overview on cloud fundamentals, and computer science students who will build cloud solutions for testing purposes.

KEYWORDS

Amazon Web Services; API; Azure; BaaS; cloud computing; computer engineering and science; Google Cloud; Java; MySQL; Node.js; SaaS; SQL

CONTENTS

LIST OF FIGURES

LIST OF TABLES

LIST OF ABBREVIATIONS

API	Application Program Interface
ASP	Application Service Providers
BSS	Business Support System
CAPEX	Capital Expenditures
CA	Certificate Authority
CPs	Cloud Providers
CSA	Cloud Security Alliance
CSU	Cloud Service Unit
CSPs	Cloud Support Providers
CRM	Customer Relation Manager
DoS	Denial of Service
DdoS	Distributed Denial of Service
EDoS	Economical Denial of Sustainability
EC2	Elastic Compute Cloud
GUIs	Graphical User Interfaces
ICT	Information and Communications Technology
IaaS	Infrastructure-as-a-Service
IoT	Internet of Things
IDS	Intrusion Detection System
JRE	Java Runtime Environment
LLC	Last Level Cache
NIST	National Institute of Standards and Technology
NoT	Network of Things
OPEX	Operating Expenses
PI	Personal Information
PII	Personally Identifiable Information
PaaS	Platform-as-a-Service
PDP	Provable Data Ownership
QoS	Quality of Service
SLA	Service Level Agreement
SOA	Service-Oriented Architecture

SDN	Software Defined Media
SaaS	Software-as-a-Service
VDI	Virtual Desktop Infrastructure
VM	Virtual Machine
VPC	Virtual Private Cloud
VPN	Virtual Private Network
VSMM	Virtual Swap Management Mechanism

ACKNOWLEDGMENTS

First and foremost, I would like to thank my family and friends for always standing by me. I also thank Nigel Wyatt, Michael Weiss (Griffith College Dublin), Gabriel Grecco (photography), and the Momentum Press team for the support and inspiration.

INTRODUCTION

This first volume of my series of works dedicated to Data Security in Cloud Computing acts as a professional benchmark, as well as a practitioner's guide to today's most complete and concise view of cloud computing security. It offers coverage on cloud computing security concepts, technology, and practice as they relate to based technologies, and to recent advancements. It investigates practical answers to a wide assortment of cloud computing protection issues.

The primary audience for this book consists of engineers/students interested in monitoring and analyzing specific, measurable cloud computing protection environments, which may include infrastructure or transportation systems, mechanical systems, seismic events, and underwater environments. This book will also be useful for safety and related professionals interested in tactical surveillance and mobile cloud computing protection target classification and monitoring. This thorough reference and practitioner's short book is also of significance to students in upper-division undergraduate and graduate-level classes in cloud computing security.

CHAPTER 1

CLOUD COMPUTING ESSENTIALS

Though the Internet was created in the 1960s, it was only in the 1990s that the potential of the Internet to serve businesses was discovered, which then led to more innovation in this area. As the transfer rates of the Internet and connectivity got better, it led to fresh types of businesses called Application Service Providers (ASPs). Consumers would pay a monthly fee to the ASPs to conduct their companies' businesses over the net from the ASP's systems. It was only in the late 1990s that cloud computing as we know it now appeared and led to the blog on what is cloud computing.

Now that we have a reasonable idea of what the cloud is, just consider all your everyday activities on the Internet, and you will understand that many of the work that you do online relies on the cloud, for example, your social networking interactions, whatever you shop online, paying your energy bills online, Internet shopping, everything is on the cloud. There is this program called the Customer Relationship Management (CRM) which relies on the cloud. This software is highly utilized in most sales organizations for superior agility, increased productivity, and low expenses. The way the cloud is used is similar to a field sales representative given access to your mobile device, which is connected to the web. He can then retrieve client information from any location. The sales representative can update the information on the move, so there is no need for him to return to the office to upgrade the information. The sales managers can also monitor everything on their web-enabled devices and will understand which deals to close.

On another note, a European cloud user who keeps their database using a cloud supplier in the United States might find that their information is subject to review because of U.S. Patriot Act. The principal benefits of cloud computing are ease of use and price reduction. Cloud suppliers specialize in the support that they provide: leasing hardware, operating systems, storage, and application services. Thus, a business does not have to engage the services of an assortment of IT employees and can concentrate on its central mission. As an example, a company does not need to have employees specialized in backup because it can buy this service from an organization that specializes in backup services like Code42 CrashPlan. The backup cloud supplier will probably offer far greater support than ad hoc employees hired to look after it. Another advantage this computing outsourcing version provides is that it reduces business expenses up front and ongoing expenses. Cloud computing providers function in a hi-tech version, eliminating burdensome tasks such as software and equipment updates and maintenance. The cloud user can use the cash saved in future gear investments and management on regions strategic to its assignment.

The National Institute of Standards and Technology (NIST; Knight 2012) has made attempts to offer a unified means to specify cloud computing from the very beginning. Despite its sophistication and complex character, NIST has identified five fundamental characteristics that signify a cloud computing system:

1. **On-demand self-service:** A consumer can unilaterally provision computing capabilities, such as server time and network storage, as needed automatically without requiring human interaction with each service provider.

2. **Broad network access:** Capabilities are available over the network and accessed through standard mechanisms that promote use by heterogeneous thin or thick client platforms (e.g., smartphones, mobile devices, tablets, laptops, and workstations).

3. **Resource pooling:** The provider's computing resources are pooled to serve multiple consumers using a multitenant model, with different physical and virtual resources dynamically assigned and reassigned according to consumer demand. There is a sense of location independence in that the customer generally has no control or knowledge over the exact location of the provided resources but may be able to specify location at a higher level of abstraction (e.g., country, state, or data center). Examples of resources include storage, processing, memory, and network bandwidth.

4. **Rapid elasticity:** Capabilities can be elastically provisioned and released, in some cases automatically, to scale rapidly outward and inward commensurate with demand. To the consumer, the capabilities available for provisioning often appear to be unlimited and can be appropriated in any quantity at any time.

5. **Measured service:** Cloud systems automatically control and optimize resource use by leveraging a metering capability at some level of abstraction appropriate to the type of service (e.g., storage, processing, bandwidth, and active user accounts). Resource usage can be monitored, controlled, and reported, providing transparency for the provider and consumer.

Resource allocation may be corrected as a client needs more (or less) storage or servers. Essentially, cloud elasticity involves continual reconfiguration in a system and relevant controls in the cloud web. The NIST distinguishes two forms of scaling alternatives: vertical and horizontal, which involve establishing added resources or services, and changing the computing capability of delegated resources, respectively.

Vertical scaling entails altering the computing capability assigned to sources while maintaining the same number of physical machines.

Virtualization enables the creation of virtual machines, software programs, and tools that serve numerous tenants in precisely the same time, rendered in the same physical infrastructure. From the cloud environment, computing tools are distant and introduced to cloud customers as a virtualized resource. When a cloud user buys access to any hardware platform, access is not provided to a real dedicated hardware but to a digital platform. Other cloud applications like Google Docs can also be shared among several cloud customers. Data is isolated from one another, similar to procedures being isolated between individuals in contemporary operating systems. Cloud computing solutions are supplied on a pay-per-use model and adhere to a "measured-service" version. The cloud supplier checks or measures the supply of solutions for a variety of reasons, including charging effective utilization of tools or general predictive preparation. Different usage-specific metrics (network I/O, storage area utilization, etc.) are used to compute fees for customers.

Cloud users access cloud tools through cloud customer software which can be installed in many different assumptions (buildings of their business) and devices (desktops, notebooks, tablet computers, and tablets).

Cloud computing contains quite a few implementations depending on the services they supply, from program service provisioning to utility and grid computing. Below we discuss about the many popular versions underlying the cloud paradigm.

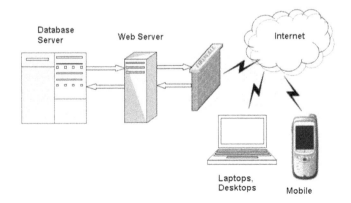

Figure 1.1. Database server, web server, internet

Figure 1.2 illustrates these three versions, which will be explained in the next subsections.

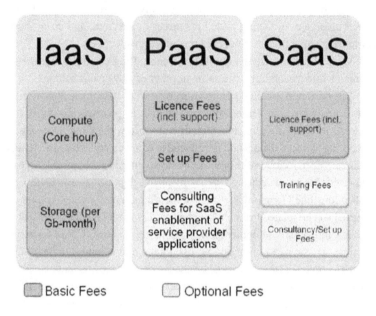

Figure 1.2. IaaS, PaaS, SaaS

1.1. INFRASTRUCTURE-AS-A-SERVICE

In this version, raw IT tools like storage, hardware, IP addresses, and firewalls are supplied to the cloud customers over the Internet. Cloud users have the freedom to set up an environment on these platforms along with the applications they need and control these tools along with their safety and dependability.

1.2. PLATFORM-AS-A-SERVICE

For cloud customers who need a more substantial degree of computing and management outsourcing, cloud suppliers also offer ready-to-use platforms as support. Within this version, an entire virtualized environment using a working system image installed may be leased. Having obtained a particular platform, cloud users are free to set up and manage software running on the virtualized environment. The amount of control and governance within the machine also reduces, since the cloud supplier installs, administers, and supports the system. The cloud supplier's policies and mechanics determine safety of hardware and operating system (OS) degree.

1.3. SOFTWARE-AS-A-SERVICE

The most populous shipping model is when a restricted number of users access third-party applications via the Internet. The cloud user has little control over how the cloud applications run along with the safety of the information it accesses. The cloud program supplier takes on all of the administrative burdens.

1.4. DEPLOYMENT DESIGNS

The way cloud providers are set up might vary based on the possession of this service—the dimensions of the cloud tools, as well as the constraints to customer access. There are three main versions: private, public, and hybrid.

Everything works as though the company outsourced the support of provisioning IT tools, environments, and applications to an off-premises third party. Inside this environment, many diverse users or organizations might interact with a physical source, such as, for instance, a server, through multitenancy and virtualization. Safety is challenging since cloud customers are determined by the cloud supplier to ensure the isolation of information and computation among a heterogeneous group of customers. An organization owns a personal cloud (Figure 1.4), situated on a server, and provides a group of IT tools to several sections or departments of the business. It centralizes IT tools in large businesses so that its different components experience all of the benefits of cloud computing: on-demand flexibility and scalability.

The company is at precisely the same time a cloud supplier and a cloud customer. Being a cloud supplier, the company assumes all of the expenses of capacity planning on any IT asset, including the load of resource management, and reliability and safety assurances. This raises the amount of security and control of business assets since they may ascertain and apply their security and company policies. After all, when files, programs, and other data are not kept securely onsite, how can they be protected?

A hybrid (Figure 1.5) shows a joint set of private and public cloud, for example, an organization may have a private cloud to store sensitive intellectual property information but may take advantage of cloud support to let servers conduct performance-intensive jobs or just because the personal cloud is operating at peak capacity. The organization should employ a protected protocol for communications between the cloud surroundings.

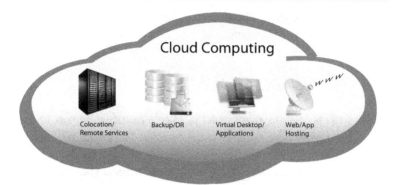

Figure 1.3. A public cloud is available to the public

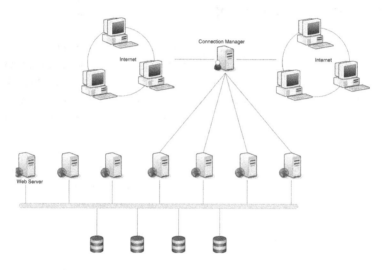

Figure 1.4. A personal cloud usually belongs to an organization

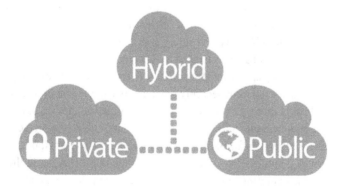

Figure 1.5. Hybrid cloud

On the other hand, the technology behind cloud computing is not wholly new. Virtualization, information outsourcing, and distant computation have been developed over the past four decades, and cloud computing systems offer a compact manner of provisioning and providing such services to clients. On this aspect, cloud computing has frequently been touted as representing a new fad, instead of being known as advanced computing technology. Therefore, it's often best described as a company paradigm as opposed to any particular technology. Within this chapter, we provide a summary of essential concepts and enabling technology of cloud computing systems such as virtualization, load balancing, tracking, scalability, and endurance. Intuitively, virtualization is an integral enabler for high server usage and multitenancy.

A cloud user, when buying access to a hardware platform, does not have access to real dedicated hardware, but to a digital platform. Like cloud applications, other sources such as Google Docs or DropBox can also be shared among several cloud users. Users are isolated from one another, similar to procedures being isolated from one individual in contemporary operating systems (Figure 1.6). Isolation methods aim at

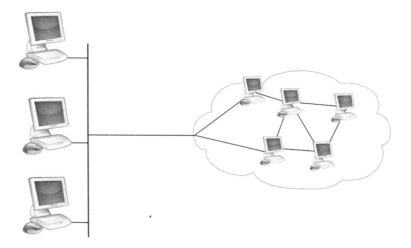

Figure 1.6. Cloud isolation

ensuring the digital surroundings residing on precisely the same node or hypervisor do not interfere with each other and shield themselves from potential pollution because of malware or data leakage. These techniques are at the center of cotenancy and therefore are helpful in controlling and maintaining multitenants independently and in isolation. Some researchers have noticed the way that isolation of virtual tools remains an open challenge (Zhang et al. 2011; Kim, Peinado, and Mainar-Ruiz 2012). According to Raj et al. (2009), tools that might be implicitly shared among VMs (vitual machines), like the last level cache (LLC) on multicore chips and memory bandwidth, are a hindrance to current levels for safety or functionality. Some have indicated a potential alternative for future cloud computing environments is to add security and functionality isolation limitations as part of the service level agreement (SLA) to boost transparency of cloud tools (Figure 1.7).

Figure 1.7. Hybrid computing environments are device agnostic when linked with cloud safely

Though businesses have mutual connections and arrangements set up, the application and data functionality might be sensitive and crucial to their business requirements.

Load balancing involves logical or physical entities responsible for distributing computational or network tasks across numerous servers to meet network and application workloads. Frequent kinds of load balancing are all round-robin, priority-based, very low latency, and so on. Together with load-balancing approaches come replication techniques. Replication techniques offer a means to keep several copies of the information in the cloud and might be host-based or even network-based. Cloud-based replication approaches offer replication of information in many places, in a load-balanced and quick method way. Specifically, replication can be employed as among many services provided to cloud customers, which may replicate their local information for greater business continuity and quicker recovery in the event of disasters at a cost-effective method.

There are lots of avenues for study, fueled by the growing fascination with cloud computing for a paradigm, a business design, and the way it affects end users and companies of any size (Cito et al. 2014).

Till date, there are tracks of academic conventions devoted to several aspects of the cloud. How does the cloud aid in answering research questions that are difficult?

Can data-intensive programs offer answers and knowledge that may open new frontiers of their understanding? Even though this is a most critical driver for study and development of grid computing architectures, it's still uncertain how to optimally function a cloud platform in certain domains, such as engineering and physics.

Also, how can large-scale computation be attained in a trusted and effective manner? The entire body of work dedicated to high-performance computing attempts to continually enhance for efficient and powerful computational and parallel processing units (Keahey et al. 2008). Secondly, what are the methods to boost cloud architecture and services?

Can cloud computing scale up for a significant amount of consumers employing a consistently transparent yet dependable method? According to Barker et al. (2014), there are a few critical opportunities for study in cloud computing which need further exploration, for example, PaaS integrations, and enhanced tools to encourage large-scale and elasticity debugging. Finally, how do we enhance cloud adopters' security (Weins 2015) and restrict potential dangers from using cloud solutions? Some recent data have shown users' hesitation in embracing clouds because of lack of assurance in the safety provided by cloud suppliers, and particularly inadequate transparency (Clarke 2017). Issues reported by consumers include lack of confidentiality, bad ethics warranties, and possibly restricted accessibility.

Even though a standardization effort is presently in place, a lot of work still needs to be done to specify cloud computing in a coherent and unified way. Interestingly, though initially considered only a buzzword by most users that were skeptical, over the past few decades the cloud has revealed to be an integral enabler for many businesses and associations, because of its flexibility and one of a kind capability to function in a tailored and cost-effective method. There are still several areas of cloud computing involving technical and less technical problems, including parallelization or pricing strategies that are worthy of analysis. Specifically, security and privacy issues continue to be significant hurdles hindering cloud adoption. A cloud host's full-time job is to carefully monitor security, which is significantly more efficient than a conventional in-house system, where an organization must divide its efforts between a myriad of IT concerns, with security being only one of them. And while most businesses don't like to openly consider the possibility of internal data theft, the truth is that a staggeringly high percentage of data thefts occur internally and are perpetrated by employees. When this is the case, it can actually be much safer to keep sensitive information off-site. Given a developing competitive marketplace, most cloud suppliers concentrate on making services scalable and practical, often preceding problems of reliability and resiliency.

REFERENCES

Barker, A., B. Varghese, J. Stuart Ward, and I. Sommerville. 2014. Academic Cloud Computing Research: Five Pitfalls and Five Opportunities. *6th USENIX Workshop on Hot Topics in Cloud Computing*. Philadelphia, PA: USENIX Association.

Cito, J., P. Leitner, T. Fritz, and H.C. Gall. 2014. The Making of Cloud Applications: An Empirical Study on Software Development for the Cloud. *Proceedings of the 2015 10th Joint Meeting on Foundations of Software Engineering*, pp. 393–403. New York, NY: ACM.

Clarke, R. 2017. Computing Clouds on the Horizon? Benefits and Risks from the User's Perspective. Private Cloud for College: Architecture and Possibility. http://ijcsn.org/IJCSN-2017/6-4/Private-Cloud-for-College-Architecture-and-Possibility.pdf

Code42 CrashPlan. http://www.code42.com/crashplan

Keahey, K., R. Figueiredo, J. Fortes, T. Freeman, and M. Tsugawa. 2008. *Science Clouds: Early Experiences in Cloud Computing for Scientific Applications*. Gainesville, FL: Cloud Computing and Applications, pp. 825–30.

Kim, T., M. Peinado, and G. Mainar-Ruiz. 2012. STEALTHMEM: System-level Protection Against Cache-based Side Channel Attacks in the Cloud. *USENIX Security Symposium*. Berkeley, CA: USENIX Association.

Raj, H., R. Nathuji, A. Singh, and P. England. 2009. Resource Management for Isolation Enhanced Cloud Services. *Proceedings of the 2009 ACM Workshop on Cloud Computing Security*. Chicago, IL: ACM.

Weins, K. 2015. Cloud Computing Trends: 2015 State of the Cloud Survey. http://www.rightscale.com/blog/cloud-industry-insights/cloud-computing-trends-2015-state-cloud-survey

Zhang, Y., A. Juels, A. Oprea, and M.K. Reiter. 2011. HomeAlone: Co-residency Detection in the Cloud via Side-channel Analysis. *2011 IEEE Symposium on Security and Privacy (SP)*. Berkeley, CA: IEEE.

CHAPTER 2

OVERVIEW OF CLOUD COMPUTING

Even though the general theories for cloud computing date back to the 1950s, cloud computing solutions specifically targeted at large businesses became available in the early 2000s. Ever since that time, cloud computing systems have spread to small- and medium-size companies, and most recently to customers.

Apple's iCloud was established in 2012 and also had twenty million consumers over a week of launching. Evernote, the cloud-based archiving and note-taking service founded in 2008 approached one hundred million consumers within six decades. This chapter starts with a more sophisticated look at the fundamental theories of cloud computing systems followed by a discussion of the main kinds of services typically provided by Cloud Providers (CPs). A consideration of both these unique models provides insight into the disposition of computing.

NIST defines cloud computing systems, in NIST SP-800-145 (National Institute of Standards and Technology 2011), as follows: "Cloud computing: A version for empowering ubiquitous, handy, on-demand community access into a shared pool of configurable computing tools (e.g., networks, servers, storage, software, and solutions) that may be quickly provisioned and introduced with minimal direction effort or support supplier interaction." This cloud model boosts accessibility and is made up of five fundamental characteristics, three support models, and four installation versions. The definition refers to several versions and attributes, whose connection is illustrated in Figure 2.1.

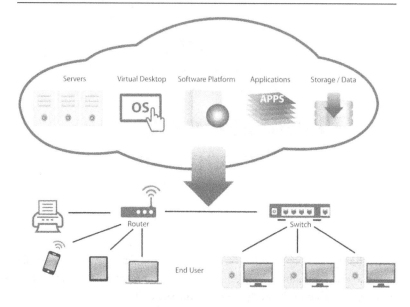

Figure 2.1. Cloud computing networks

2.1. ESSENTIAL CHARACTERISTICS

Broad network accessibility: Capabilities are offered within the network and obtained through conventional mechanisms that encourage use by heterogeneous thick or thin client platforms (e.g., cellular telephones, notebooks, and PDAs) and other conventional or cloud-based applications services.

Quick elasticity: Cloud computing provides you with the capacity to manage funds based on your particular service requirements. As an example, you might require many host tools for the duration of a particular job. After that, you can release these resources on completion of the job.

Measured support: Cloud systems mechanically control and maximize resource usage by metering capability at some level of abstraction appropriate to the sort of job/task (e.g., storage, computing, calculating, and busy user accounts).

On-demand self-evident: A user can supply computing services, for example, server network and time storage, mechanically as needed without requiring human interaction with every service provider.

Resource pooling: The supplier's computing tools are set to function for numerous customers utilizing a multitenant version, with distinct virtual and physical tools easily configured and assigned based on customer demand. There's a level of place independence in the client that has typically no knowledge or control within the precise place of the supplied resources but might have the ability to specify a place in a higher level of abstraction (e.g., nation, country, or information center). Even personal clouds often pool funds between various areas of the same business.

Figure 2.2 illustrates the normal cloud support circumstance. An enterprise asserts workstations inside an enterprise LAN or collection of LANs, which can be connected by a modem using a network or the World Wide Web into the cloud supplier. The cloud support provider maintains a massive selection of servers, which it handles with many different network controls, redundancy, and security gear. The figure of the cloud infrastructure reveals a selection of blade servers, which can also be configured as standard architecture.

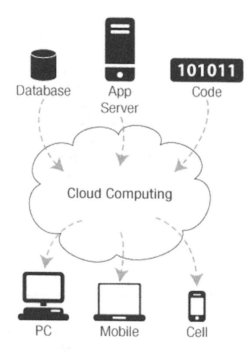

Figure 2.2. Cloud support

2.2. CLOUD SERVICES

Figure 2.3 compares the functions executed by the cloud support supplier for the three main cloud supported versions. All these are universally accepted as the fundamental service models for computing. The section discusses these versions and examines other popular cloud support versions.

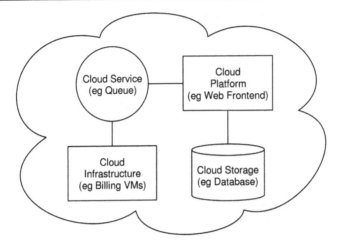

Figure 2.3. Compares the functions executed by the cloud support supplier for the three main cloud support versions

As its name suggests, a SaaS cloud offers support to clients in the kind of applications, namely, application software, operating on and reachable from the cloud. SaaS empowers the client to utilize the CP's software running on the supplier's cloud infrastructure. The applications are available from several client devices via a simple interface like an Internet browser. Rather than getting server and desktop licenses for software products it uses, an organization gets the very same functions from the cloud support.

Frequent contributors to SaaS are companies that are looking to supply their workers with standard office productivity applications, such as file management and e-mail. Users also typically utilize the SaaS model to obtain cloud tools. Usually, readers utilize particular applications when they need them. The CP also generally offers data-related features like automatic backup and information sharing between readers. The next list, based on a continuous business survey by OpenCrowd, clarifies instances of SaaS services:

- **Billing:** Application services to control customer billing based on subscriptions and usage to goods and solutions.
- **Collaboration:** Utilities supply tools that enable consumers to collaborate within workgroups, inside businesses, and across businesses.
- **Content management:** Services for handling the manufacturing and access to articles for Internet-based software.
- **Document direction:** Platforms for handling files, record creation workflows, and supplying workspaces for classes or businesses to access and find files.

- **Instruction:** Providers of Internet services to teachers and educational institutions.
- **Financials:** Software for handling financial procedures for businesses which vary from processing expenditures and invoicing to taxation administration.
- **Health care:** Services for enhancing and managing people's well-being, and health care administration.
- **IT solutions management:** Software that helps businesses manage IT services from shipping to solutions for customers, and also to manage performance development.
- **Personal Improvement:** Software that company users employ on a daily basis in the regular course of business.
- **Project direction:** Software bundles for handling projects. Characteristics of bundles may include specialized supplies for certain kinds of jobs like applications development and structure.
- **Revenue:** Software that is mainly created for sales purposes like pricing and commission monitoring.
- **Security:** Hosted goods for safety services like virus and malware scanning, and only sign-on.
- **Social networks:** Platforms for customizing and creating social media programs.

2.3. PLATFORM-AS-A-SERVICE AND IAAS

A Platform as a Service or PaaS cloud offers support to clients in the stage where the client's need is to cooperate using an "out-of-the-box" type solution. PaaS empowers the client to deploy on the cloud infrastructure customer-created or obtained applications.

A PaaS cloud offers useful software building blocks, and numerous development applications, for example, programming language resources, runtime environments, along with other tools which help in deploying new software. PaaS is helpful for a company that wishes to create new or straightforward software while focusing on the computing resources only if required.

The following listing clarifies example PaaS providers:

- Platforms for the development of business intelligence software such as dashboards, reporting programs, and significant data analysis.
- Scalable database programs, which vary from relational database alternatives to hugely scalable NoSQL datastores.

- Platforms just for the testing and development cycles of program development, which expand and contract as necessary.
- Platforms suited to general purpose program development.
- Services for incorporating software which ranges from cloud-to-cloud integration to custom program integration.

In the case of IaaS or Infrastructure as a Service, we have a solution that offers virtual machines along with additional curricular hardware and operating systems. IaaS delivers the consumer processing, networks, storage, along with other necessary computing tools so the customer can deploy and run the custom software, which may include things such as operating systems and software. IaaS empowers customers to unite standard computing solutions, including number crunching and data storage, to construct highly flexible PC systems.

The following list clarifies illustration IaaS services:

- **Cloud agent:** Applications that manage services over one cloud infrastructure system; a few tools encourage personal–people cloud configurations.
- **Compute:** Provides host tools for conducting cloud-based systems which could be provisioned and configured as required.
- **Content delivery networks (CDNs):** CDNs store material and documents to enhance the operation and price of delivering articles for online systems.
- **Services direction:** Services that handle cloud infrastructure systems. These tools frequently provide attributes that CPs do not supply or focus in handling specific application technology.
- **Storage:** Provides highly scalable storage capability, which may be used for programs, archiving, backups, document storage, and much more.

2.4. ADDITIONAL CLOUD SERVICES

- **Communications as an agency (CaaS):** The integration of real-time discussion and cooperation solutions to maximize business processes. This support provides a unified interface and is also composed of consumer experiences across multiple devices.
- **Compute as an agency (CompaaS):** The supply and use of processing tools necessary to deploy and operate applications.
- **Data storage for support (DSaaS):** The supply and use of information storage and relevant capabilities. DSaaS refers to a storage version where the customer leases storage distance from a third-party

supplier. Data are transferred from the customer to the service provider through the net, and the customer then gets the saved information using software supplied by the storage supplier. The computer software is utilized to execute everyday tasks associated with storage, like data backups and data transfers.

- **Network as an agency (NaaS)**: Provides transportation connectivity solutions or intercloud network connectivity solutions. NaaS requires the optimization of resource allocations by contemplating computing and network tools as a unified whole.

Recommendation Y.3500 (08/14) differentiates between cloud capacities and cloud solutions. A cloud support class may contain capacities from a couple of cloud capacity types.

- **Database as an agency:** Database functionalities are based on demand for which the cloud supplier has done the set up and maintenance of the databases.
- **Desktop as an agency:** Provides the capability to construct, configure, manage, save, implement, and send users' desktop capabilities remotely. Essentially, a desktop computer provides a service offload shared desktop programs plus sends data from the user's desktop computer or notebook computer to the cloud, and is also designed to provide a reliable, consistent experience for its distant use of applications, programs, procedures, and documents.
- **E-mail as a service:** Offers an entire e-mail service along with related services like storage, reception, transmission, backup, and retrieval of e-mail.
- **Identity for support:** Identity and access management which may be extended and concentrated into existing working environments including provisioning, directory management, as well as the performance of one sign-on support.
- **Security as an agency:** The integration of a suite of security solutions within the present working environment by the cloud supplier.

2.5. XAAS (ANYTHING-AS-A-SERVICE)

XaaS is the most recent development in the supply of CPs. The acronym contains three generally accepted interpretations, all of which pretty much mean the exact same thing:

- **Anything for a service:** Where "whatever" identifies any service aside from the three traditional services.

- **Everything for a service:** Though this variant is occasionally spelled out, it is somewhat misleading because no seller provides every potential cloud support. This version is supposed to imply that the cloud support supplier is giving a vast assortment of service offerings.
- **X for support:** Here X could represent any potential cloud support alternative.

XaaS suppliers go beyond the conventional "big three" (Software as a Service [SaaS], Platform as a Service [PaaS] and Infrastructure as a Service [IaaS]) providers in three ways:

- Some XaaS suppliers package SaaS, PaaS, and IaaS collectively, so the client can perform a one-stop search for the first cloud solution which businesses are coming to rely upon.
- XaaS suppliers can progressively displace a more extensive selection of services which IT departments typically provide internal clients. This approach reduces the burden on the IT department to obtain, preserve, patch, and update some standard applications and solutions.
- The XaaS model generally involves a continuing relationship between client and supplier, where you will find regular status updates along with a real two-way, real-time exchange of support and information exchange.

As a consequence, this can be a managed service that allows the client to commit to just the total amount of service required at any moment and to expand the quantity and forms of service when the client's requirements increase.

1. Total costs are controlled and decreased. By executing the full assortment of IT services into a skilled specialist spouse, a business sees both long-term and immediate price reductions. Capital costs are drastically reduced because the requirement for hardware is much less and applications are locally procured. Operating expenses are reduced as the tools utilized are tailored to instant needs and change just as demands change.
2. This removes the risks of cost overruns so prevalent with inner jobs. The usage of one supplier for a broad selection of services provides one point of contact for resolving issues.
3. Innovation is hastened: IT departments always run the risk of installing new hardware and applications only to discover that later variants which are more competent, less costly, or both are

accessible from the time setup is complete. Together with XaaS, the hottest offerings are more rapidly accessible. Further, suppliers can respond quickly to consumer feedback.

There's an increasingly prominent tendency in several businesses to move a significant portion or all IT operations to business cloud computing. The organization is confronted with a selection of options as to cloud possession and direction. This segment looks at the four prominent deployment models for computing.

2.6.   PUBLIC CLOUD

Public cloud infrastructure is made accessible to the general public or a large business group and is owned by an organization promoting cloud solutions. The CP is responsible both for its cloud infrastructure and also for the management of information and operations inside the cloud. It is dependent upon the assumptions of this cloud supplier. At a public cloud version, all significant components are beyond the enterprise firewall, situated at a multitenant infrastructure. Storage and applications are all made accessible over the web via procured IP and may be free or provided in a pay-per-usage charge. This kind of cloud provides easy-to-use consumer-type providers, for example, Amazon and Google on-demand net applications or capability, Yahoo e-mail, and Facebook or LinkedIn social websites supplying free storage for photos. While cloud users setup are cheap and scale to fulfill demands, they generally offer no (or less extensive) service level agreements (SLAs) and might not provide the guarantees against information corruption or loss found with hybrid or private offerings. Public cloud is proper for entities and consumers not requiring the very same levels of support which are anticipated inside the firewall.

Additionally, the public IaaS clouds do not automatically provide for limitations and compliance with all privacy legislation, which remain the responsibility of the contributor or corporate end user. Examples of providers here could be picture and audio sharing, notebook backup, or document sharing. The significant benefit of this public cloud is the price. A subscribing company pays for the resources and services it requires and can correct these as needed. What's more, the subscriber will have considerably reduced management overheads.

The primary concern is safety; nonetheless, there are quite a few people CPs who have shown strong security controls and, in actuality, such suppliers may have more tools and expertise to devote to safety that would be offered in a cloud.

2.7. PERSONAL CLOUD

A personal cloud is employed inside the inner IT environment of a business. The company might opt to deal with the cloud in-house or contract the management function to a third party. Personal clouds may provide IaaS internally to workers or business units via an intranet or the Internet using a VPN, in addition to applications (software) or storage as solutions to its division offices. Examples of solutions delivered via the personal cloud comprise a database on demand, e-mail on demand, and storage on demand.

A necessary motivation for choosing a personal cloud is safety. Personal cloud infrastructure provides tighter controls within the geographical location of information storage and other elements of security. Other advantages include simple resource sharing and quick installation to organizational entities.

2.8. COMMUNITY CLOUD

A community cloud stocks features of public and private clouds. Just like a personal cloud, a community cloud has limited access. Just like a public cloud, the community cloud tools are shared among numerous independent businesses. The organizations that utilize the community cloud have comparable conditions and, usually, a need to exchange information with one another. One example of a business that is employing the community cloud theory is the health care market. The community participants can swap information in a controlled manner.

The cloud infrastructure might be handled by the participating organizations or even by a third party and might exist on or off the premises. In this deployment model, the costs will be spread over fewer consumers than the usual public cloud (however, more than the usual personal cloud); therefore, just some of their cost savings potential for cloud computing will be realized.

2.9. HYBRID

The hybrid infrastructure is a composition of a couple of clouds (personal, community, or users that stay exceptional entities but are bound together by proprietary or standardized technology that permits information and program reliability). Using a hybrid solution, sensitive data can be put in a private region of the cloud and not as sensitive information can benefit from the advantages of the cloud. A hybrid public/private cloud option can be especially attractive for smaller companies.

Many programs for which safety issues are less of a problem could be offloaded at substantial cost savings without committing the company to transfer more sensitive information and software to the public cloud.

Table 2.1. Comparison of cloud deployment

Public	Community	Private	Hybrid
Off premise at provider	On or off premise	On or off premise	On or off premise
General public	Multiple, related organizations	Limited to a single organization	Determined by each cloud
Users' concerns and purposes vary	Users share the same concerns	Used by various business units	Users' concerns and purposes vary

NIST SP 500-292 (National Institute of Standards and Technology 2011) builds a benchmark structure, explained as follows:

The NIST cloud computing reference architecture concentrates on the needs of "that which" CPs supply, maybe not a "how to" style solution and execution. The reference structure is meant to ease the understanding of the operational intricacies of computing. It doesn't signify the system structure of a particular cloud computing platform; instead, it's a tool for describing, discussing, and creating a system-specific architecture employing a standard frame of reference.

NIST developed the benchmark structure together with the following aims in mind:

- To exemplify and understand the variety of cloud solutions from the context of a general cloud computing conceptual design.
- To supply a technical benchmark for consumers to understand, talk, categorize, and compare cloud hosting solutions.
- To ease the evaluation of candidate criteria for safety, interoperability, and reliability and reference implementations.

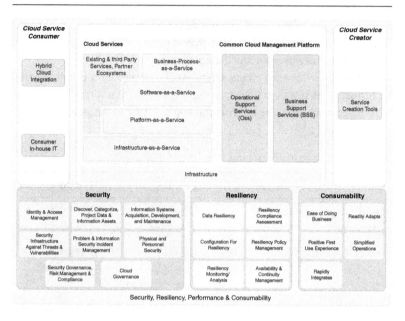

Figure 2.4. Four primary architectural components of the CP (user, supplier, auditor, agent)

The reference structure, depicted in Figure 2.4, defines five big "actors" concerning the functions and responsibilities as described in the listing that follows:

- **Cloud user:** An individual or company that keeps a business relationship with, and utilizes service out of, CPs.
- **Cloud supplier:** An individual, company, or entity responsible for creating a service available to interested parties.
- **Cloud auditor:** It runs the individual assessment of cloud solutions, data system operations, functionality, and safety of the cloud execution.
- **Cloud agent:** An entity that manages the usage, functionality, and shipping of cloud solutions, and negotiates connections between CPs and cloud customers.
- **Cloud Inc.:** An intermediary that provides transport and connectivity of cloud solutions from CPs to cloud customers.

The functions of this cloud consumer and supplier have been discussed. To summarize, a CP can supply at least one of the cloud solutions to fulfill IT and business demands of cloud customers. For all the three service versions (SaaS, PaaS, and IaaS), the CP supplies the processing and storage facilities required to support the service version, together with a cloud port for cloud support customers. For SaaS that the CP deploys, it configures, maintains, and upgrades the performance of their software programs on cloud infrastructure, so the services are provisioned in the anticipated service amounts to cloud customers.

The customers of SaaS may be organizations that offer their members using applications, software applications, or applications program administrators who configure software for end users. For PaaS, the CP oversees the computing infrastructure to its platform and conducts the cloud applications that offer the parts of the platform, including runtime program implementation heap, databases, and other middleware components. Cloud users of PaaS can use the resources and implementation resources supplied by CPs to create, install, test, and manage the software hosted on a cloud atmosphere. For IaaS, the CP accelerates the computing tools underlying the support, such as the servers, storage, networks, and hosting infrastructure.

The IaaS cloud user consequently employs these computing tools, like computer, for their necessary computing requirements. The cloud provider is a media facility that offers transport and connectivity of cloud solutions between cloud customers and CPs. Usually, a CP will install SLAs using a cloud provider to provide services following the degree of SLAs provided to cloud customers and might require the cloud provider to offer secure and dedicated connections between cloud customers and CPs. A cloud agent is helpful when CPs are too complicated to get a cloud user to handle readily. A cloud agent could offer two regions of service:

- **Service aggregation:** The agent combines multiple cloud solutions to fulfill customer needs not addressed explicitly with one CP, to maximize performance, or to decrease cost.
- **Service arbitrage:** This is much like support aggregation except that the professional services being aggregated are not fixed. Support arbitrage means a broker has the flexibility to select services from several agencies. As an example, the cloud agent could utilize credit-scoring support to quantify and pick a service using the best score.

A cloud auditor may assess the services offered using a CP concerning security controllers, privacy impact, functionality, and so on. The auditor is an independent entity which could guarantee the CP conforms to some criteria. Figure 2.5 illustrates the connections between the "actors."

A cloud user may ask cloud solutions out of a CP directly or by using a cloud agent. A cloud auditor conducts independent audits and might get in touch with others to gather necessary information. This figure demonstrates

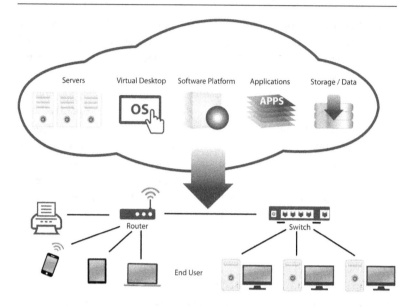

Figure 2.5. Cloud "actors" connections

that cloud networking problems involve three distinct kinds of networks. For a cloud manufacturer, the system structure is that of a standard large information center, which is made up of racks of high-performance servers and storage apparatus, connected with high-speed top-of-rack Ethernet switches. The business network is very likely to possess a different structure, typically including numerous LANs, servers, workstations, PCs, and mobile devices, using a wide selection of network functionality, safety, and management problems. The concern of the consumer and producer concerning the cloud provider, which can be shared with many customers, is the capacity to create virtual networks, together with appropriate SLAs and safety guarantees.

2.10. CLOUD PROVIDER ARCHITECTURAL COMPONENTS

Figure 2.4 shows four primary architectural components of the CP. Service orchestration denotes the composition of program components to support the CPs' actions in structure, coordination, and management of computing resources to provide cloud services to cloud consumers. The orchestration is shown as a three-layer architecture. We see here the simple mapping of physical resources to consumer-visible services by a resource abstraction layer. Examples of resource abstraction elements include software elements, for example, hypervisors, virtual machines, virtual information storage, and other computing resource abstractions. Cloud service management contains each of the service-related functions that are essential for the management and operation of those services required by or proposed to cloud customers. It covers three main areas:

Business service: This comprises business-related services dealing with clients, such as bookkeeping, billing, reporting, and auditing.

Provisioning/configuration: This includes automated tools for rapid deployment of cloud systems for customers, adjusting resource and configuration assignment, and tracking and reporting on resource usage.

Portability/interoperability: Consumers are interested in cloud offerings which encourage data and system portability, and service interoperability. This is very useful in a hybrid environment, in which the consumer may wish to alter the allocation of information and software between on-premises and off-premises sites.

Security is a concern that crosses all layers of this reference architecture, which range from physical security to application security. As such, it is the joint responsibility of all of the cloud "actors," not only CPs. Privacy additionally encompasses all layers of this reference architecture. The critical requirement concerning privacy is that CPs provide adequate and guaranteed protection of personal information (PI) and personally identifiable information (PII) from the cloud.

2.11.   ITU-T CLOUD COMPUTING REFERENCE ARCHITECTURE

It is beneficial to check at an alternative reference structure, published in ITU-T Y.3502 (International Telecommunication Union 2014). This architecture is somewhat broader in scope compared to NIST structure and views it as a layered functional architecture.

2.11.1.   CLOUD COMPUTING "ACTORS"

Before taking a look at the four-layer benchmark architecture, we need to understand the differences between NIST and ITU-T in defining cloud "actors." The ITU-T document defines the three "actors" as follows:

- **Cloud support customer or consumer:** A party that is in a business relationship to utilize cloud solutions. The business relationship is using a cloud service provider or a cloud support spouse.

Critical actions for a cloud support customer include but are not limited to, utilizing cloud solutions, performing company administration, and administering utilization of cloud solutions.

- **Cloud service supplier:** A party that produces cloud services out there. The cloud service provider targets tasks that are necessary to provide a cloud service and actions that are necessary to ensure its delivery to the cloud service customer in addition to cloud support maintenance. The cloud service provider includes a comprehensive set of activities (e.g., provide service, deploy and track service, handle business plan, provide audit information, etc.) as well as many sub-roles (e.g., company manager, service manager, network provider, security and risk manager, and the like).

- **Cloud service partner:** A party that is engaged in service of, or auxiliary to, activities of either the cloud service provider or the cloud service client, or even both. A cloud service spouse's activities vary depending on the kind of spouse and their relationship with the cloud service provider and the cloud service customer. Cases of cloud service partners include cloud auditor and cloud support agent.

Therefore, the cloud service spouse combines but is not limited to, the NIST functions of agent and auditor. Figure 2.6 depicts the main "actors" with some of their possible characters in a cloud ecosystem.

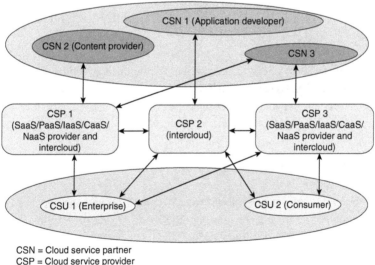

CSN = Cloud service partner
CSP = Cloud service provider
CSU = Cloud service user

Figure 2.6. Cloud ecosystem

2.11.2. LAYERED ARCHITECTURE

The user layer is the user interface whereby a cloud support client interacts with a cloud hosting supplier and with cloud services, performs customer-related administrative tasks, and monitors cloud hosting services. It can also offer the output of cloud services to another resource layer case.

After the cloud receives support requests, it orchestrates its assets and other clouds' resources (if other clouds' tools are obtained via the intercloud purpose) and supplies back cloud solutions through the user coating. The user layer is where the cloud service unit (CSU) resides. The access layer provides a common interface for both manual and automatic access to the capabilities available in the services layer.

These capabilities include both the capabilities of their services and also the administration and business capabilities. The access layer takes a partner or user or alternative provider cloud service consumption requests using cloud APIs to access the supplier's services and resources.

The access layer is responsible for introducing cloud service capacities over one or more access mechanisms, such as for a set of web pages accessed via a browser, or as a set of web solutions which can be accessed programmatically. The access layer additionally deals with safety and high Quality of Service (QoS). The support layer contains the implementation of the services provided by a cloud supplier (e.g., SaaS, PaaS, IaaS).

The support layer contains and controls the software components that employ the solutions (but not the inherent hypervisors, host operating systems, device drivers, etc.), and arranges to offer the cloud services to customers through the access layer. The resource layer contains physical resources available to the provider and the proper abstraction and control mechanisms. As an example, hypervisor software might offer virtual machine, virtual storage, and virtual machine capacities. Also, it houses the cloud core transport network functionality that's required to provide built-in network connectivity between the provider and consumers. The multilayer functions include a string of functional elements that interact with practical elements of the four different layers to provide supporting capabilities. It comprises five categories of practical components:

- **Integration:** Responsible for connecting functional components in the design to make a unified architecture. The functional integration elements provide message routing and message exchange mechanisms within the cloud architecture and its functional components in addition to external functional components.
- **Security systems:** Responsible for implementing security-related controls to mitigate the security threats in cloud computing

environments. The safety systems' operational components encompass all of the security facilities required to support cloud services.

OSS is also involved in system monitoring, including the use of events and alarms.

- **Business support system (BSS):** Encompasses the set of business-related management capabilities dealing with clients and supporting processes, such as accounts and charging.
- **Development purpose:** Supports the cloud computing activities of the cloud service programmer including support of this development and of service implementations, build management, and test management.

Figure 2.7 shows the four-layer cloud computing reference architecture defined in Recommendation ITU-T Y.3502. This architecture has the same four-layer structure as that of Y.3500; however, it provides more detail of the lowest layer known as the tools and system layer. This layer consists of two sublayers.

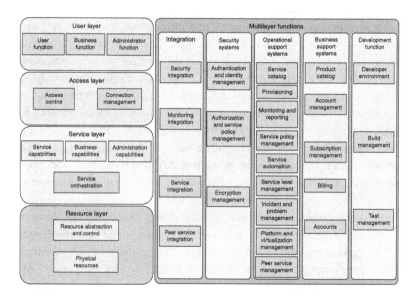

Figure 2.7. Shows the four-layer cloud computing reference architecture as described in *Cloud Computing—Overview and Vocabulary.* ITU-T Y.3500

- **Resource orchestration:** The direction, tracking, and monitoring of computing, storage, and community resources into consumable services from the upper layers and users. It controls the production, modification, and release of resources that are reconditioned.
- **Physical resources:** The computing, storage, and community resources which are fundamental to providing cloud solutions. These tools may include the ones that reside inside cloud data centers (e.g., computing servers, storage servers, and intracloud networks) and those that reside outside data centers, typically networking resources, including intercloud networks and core transport networks.

These virtual resources are subsequently managed and controlled by the source orchestration, based on consumer demand. Software and platform resources in the pooling and virtualization layer are the runtime environment, applications, and other applications assets utilized to orchestrate and implement cloud services.

2.12. NETWORK REQUIREMENTS FOR CLOUD COMPUTING

It will be helpful in this regard to consider the cloud system version developed by ITU-T and exhibited in Figure 2.8 (International Telecommunication Union 2012). This figure indicates the reach of network issues for cloud service and network providers as well as cloud service users.

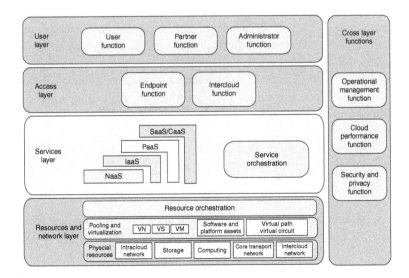

Figure 2.8. Cloud system version developed by ITU-T

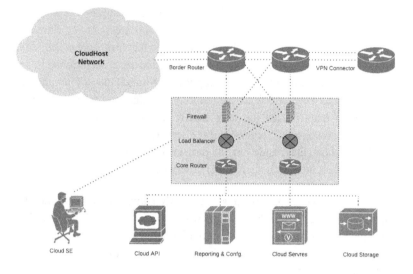

Figure 2.9. Cloud host network

A cloud support provider asserts one or more local or regional cloud infrastructures. The intracloud system will likely include some LANs connected with IP routers. Within the infrastructure, database servers have been organized as a cluster of virtual machines, providing virtualized, isolated computing environments for various users. These cloud infrastructures may be owned by precisely the same CP or from different ones. Finally, a core transport network is used by clients to access and have cloud solutions installed inside the CP's data center. The processes supported by network OSS include service management and maintenance of the network inventory, configuration of specific network elements, in addition to fault direction.

Cloud OSS: OSS of cloud computing infrastructure is the system devoted to providers of cloud computing services. Cloud OSS supports procedures for the maintenance, monitoring, and configuration of all cloud resources.

These three network elements (intracloud, intercloud, center), with the OSS components, are the base of cloud solutions composition and delivery:

- **Scalability:** Networks should have the ability to scale quickly to meet the requirements of moving from current cloud infrastructures of hundreds or a few thousand servers to networks of tens of thousands or perhaps hundreds of thousands of servers. This scaling presents challenges in areas such as addressing, routing, and congestion control.

- **Performance:** Traffic in both large data installations and CP networks is unpredictable and somewhat variable (Kandula, Sengupta, and Patel 2009). There are sustained spikes between local servers within precisely the same rack and intermittent heavy traffic using a single source server and several destination servers. Intracloud networks need to supply reliable high-speed direct (logical point-to-point) communications between servers with congestion-free connections, and uniform capability between any two random servers inside the data center. The ITU-T report concludes that the present three-tier topology (access, aggregation, and core) used in data centers is not well adapted to provide all these requirements. More flexible and dynamic control of data flows as well as virtualization of network devices provides a much better base for supplying the desired QoS.

- **Agility and flexibility:** The cloud-based data center needs to have the ability to respond and manage the highly dynamic nature of cloud resource usage. This includes the ability to adapt to virtual machine freedom and to provide fine-grained control of leaks routing through the data center.

The media requirements to encourage cloud computing systems have been one of the key driving factors in the development and deployment of new media technologies, mainly software defined media (SDN) and the system operates virtualization (Stallings 2015; Erpinnews 2017; GovernmentCIO n.d.; Cloud Computing n.d.; International Communication Union 2016; people.unica.it n.d.).

Cloud computing provides economies of scale, professional community management, and skilled security management. The individual or company only must pay for the storage capability and services that they require. The consumer, be it a business or an individual, should not have the hassle of setting up a database program, acquiring the hardware they need, performing maintenance, and backing up the data: all this is a portion of the cloud support. In theory, another huge benefit of using cloud computing to store your data and discuss it with other people is that the CP manages security. Alas, the customer is not always protected. There have been many safety failures among CPs. Evernote.com made headlines in early 2013 as it advised all of its customers to reset their passwords after an intrusion was discovered. Cloud safety is addressed in subsequent chapters.

REFERENCES

Cloud Computing. n.d. "Cloud Computing Governance Framework." http://www.opengroup.org/cloud/gov_snapshot/p6.htm

Erpinnews. 2017. "Cloud Computing Service Models." https://erpinnews.com/cloud-computing-service-models

GovernmentCIO. n.d. "Going All in with Cloud Computing." https://www.governmentcio.com/media-0International Telecommunication Union. 2012. *Focus Group on Cloud Computing. Technical*

International Telecommunication Union. 2012. *Focus Group on Cloud Computing. Technical Report. Part 3: Requirements and Framework Architecture of Cloud Infrastructure.* ITU-T FG Cloud TR. Geneva, Switzerland: International Telecommunication Union.

International Telecommunication Union. 2014. *Cloud Computing Architecture.* ITU-T Y.3502. Geneva, Switzerland: International Telecommunication Union.

International Telecommunication Union. 2014. *Cloud Computing—Overview and Vocabulary.* ITU-T Y.3500. Geneva, Switzerland: International Telecommunication Union.

International Communication Union. 2016. "Cloud Computing—Framework and High-level Requirements," ITU-T Rec. Y.3501 (06/2016). http://static.kexinyun.org/upload/T-REC.pdf

Kandula, A., S. Sengupta, and P. Patel. 2009. The Nature of Data Center Traffic: Measurements and Analysis. *ACM SIGCOMM Internet Measurement Conference*, November 4–6, Chicago, IL.

National Institute of Standards and Technology. 2011. *The NIST Cloud Computing Reference Architecture.* Special Publication SP-500-292. Gaithersburg, MD: National Institute of Standards and Technology.

National Institute of Standards and Technology. 2011. *The NIST Definition of Cloud Computing.* Special Publication SP-800-145. Gaithersburg, MD: National Institute of Standards and Technology.

people.unica.it. n.d. "Infrastrutture ed Applicazioni Avanzate," ITU-T Rec. Y.3501 (06/2016). http://people.unica.it/luigiatzori1/files/2016/09/2-Requirements.pdf

Stallings, W. 2015. *Foundations of Modern Networking: SDN, NFV, QoE, IoT, and Cloud.* Englewood Cliffs, NJ: Pearson.

CHAPTER 3

Cloud Security Baselines

3.1. FUNDAMENTALS

This chapter discusses the fundamentals of protection in cloud computing, and the principal challenges in this area. It begins with a summary of personal security, discussing its three main columns—ethics, confidentiality, and accessibility—and also other crucial concepts like credibility and trust.

This chapter also discusses the ideas of vulnerabilities, threats, and strikes generally, and, in the context of cloud computing systems, it is followed by a summary of the most common mitigations for cloud computing dangers. This chapter also talks about privacy and safety in cloud-storage solutions and multiclouds and cloud reliability.

Computer safety contains three crucial pillars, which can be remembered by using the acronym CIA, which stands for:

- Confidentiality
- Integrity
- Accessibility

Confidentiality includes the concealment of sensitive data from unauthorized parties. Three mechanisms help apply privacy. The first is cryptography, which hides plain text data using mathematical transformations. The next is access management, which defines the parties allowed access to specific areas of the machine or particular parts of information.

The last is empowerment, which decides what activities each approved party is permitted to do with a bit of information or a system module (Bishop 2003; Goodrich and Tamassia 2010; Stallings and Brown 2012). The ethics pillar means unauthorized parties cannot change a system and its data. Mechanisms protecting integrity generally attempt to defend against a change or tampering from happening in the first place or to discover an attack after it has occurred. The next column, accessibility, describes the property that a system and its information needs in order to be accessible to authorized parties in a timely way.

There are other crucial concepts like authenticity, which is about the data and transactions being real, and non-repudiation, which is the guarantee that a party cannot deny a trade, a statement, or even a touch. In computer security, we predict these flaws as vulnerabilities. Computer systems will not ever be free of vulnerabilities since they are created, implemented, and analyzed by people, who continuously make errors. A weakness is consequently a threat to safety. We predict an assault—a danger that is accomplished using an adversary, frequently exploiting at least one of a system's vulnerabilities.

The safety challenges in cloud computing systems are not too different from those in conventional computing, except that the cloud environment increases the number of vulnerabilities and the effect of strikes. Because the cloud environment contains many levels of abstraction—program, operating system, structure, and community—an attacker has a lot of paths for undermining the safety of cloud support, for instance, a vulnerability in an online cloud program that does not sanitize inputs may create the disclosure of sensitive information stored at a data center.

As we have said, cloud computing solutions can pose vulnerabilities in most layers of abstraction (Grobauer, Walloschek, and Stocker 2011). Figure 3.1 reveals cloud safety vulnerabilities in line with this layer giving an idea of where they may happen.

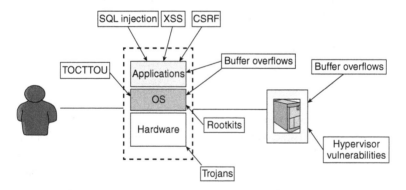

Figure 3.1. Reveals cloud safety vulnerabilities

3.2. PROGRAM LAYER

In the program level, a cloud program may have several flaws that enable a bad actor to bypass credentials verification and gather information on version of database installed. Many cloud programs are Internet based and also have classic Internet vulnerabilities like inadequate user input, which makes it possible for attacks like SQL injection (Su and Wassermann 2006). A SQL injection vulnerability allows an attacker to inject outside code into an Internet search engine to be implemented utilizing a SQL query interpreter. It is still widely reported in vulnerability databases although it has been researched because of what happened in the mid-2000s. To know that vulnerability, first, consider a typical situation of an individual interacting with a web host hosting a web application that stores its information in a database. Usually, the code to your web application and the database are saved in various machines. In a typical situation, a web application deployed employing a publication retailer (e.g., Amazon) enables users to look for books according to their author, title, and so on.

The whole book catalog stored in a database along with the program uses SQL queries to recover book details. The Internet scripting engine then constructs a SQL command that is a mixture of directions written by the program developer and the consumer input. This question causes the database to look at each row over the novels table, pull on all those documents in which the writer pillar has the value "Wiley," and return the record of all of these records.

This listing set is processed from the web application and presented to the consumer inside an HTML page. Now, think about a situation where an attacker can cause a fracture from the interpretation of this information and break from this information context. String data in SQL queries have to be encapsulated within single quote marks, to separate it in the remainder of the query. Within this situation, an attacker provides input comprising a quote mark to complete the series (') she controls, and a brand new SQL command is created changing the question that the programmer intended the program to execute. There is an open fracture in the way in which the input is translated in the border between the Internet scripting language and the SQL query interpreter.

The double hyphen -LRB----RRB- from the attacker's input informs the query interpreter to dismiss the rest of the lineup although there might be additional commands contained from the program developer. The result of this assault is the deletion of the whole "novels" table in the database as illustrated in Figure 3.2. What is more is that the program code may be vulnerable to remote code injection via buffer overflows (Lhee and Chapin. 2003) even if it's coded in a programming language that does not verify range boundaries, including C or C++.

The program could also be vulnerable to sensitive information disclosure if it does not use cryptography to keep the confidentiality of this data that it manipulates. The program code could also be susceptible to being undermined if its authentication and access control processes have defects.

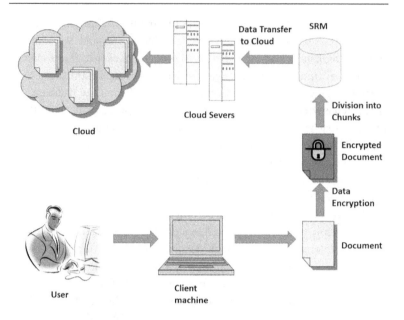

Figure 3.2. User, client machine, cloud server flow

Vulnerabilities in the operating system level may also compromise cloud safety. OSs are also vulnerable to vulnerabilities associated with race conditions, like the TOCTTOU (time of check to time of use) vulnerability.

The TOCTTOU vulnerability results from changes to a method that happens while assessing a state (like a security credential) along with the usage of the consequences of the check. TOCTTOU is made up of check stage, which determines an invariant precondition (e.g., accessibility consent), and also a use stage, which functions on the thing assuming the invariant remains legitimate. TOCTTOU (time-of-check-to-time-of-use, the class of software bugs caused by changes in a system between the condition checking and the result use of that check) generally occurs in SE-TUID (Set User ID upon execution) procedures, which have administrator privileges but may be invoked by unprivileged users; thus, the process can perform tasks on the consumer's behalf. As an example, a printing application is generally SETUID-root to get into the printer apparatus, which can be an operation that needs administrative privileges. Running like the consumer receives the root privileges, the printer application then finds if an individual invoking its implementation has permission to read and publish a specific file by using the accessibility purpose from the working system. Processes are implemented by OSs in an interleaved manner, as the OS schedules one procedure at one time on each CPU. Thus, a method does not perform at the CPU from beginning to finish without being disrupted.

The CPU implements a technique for some period, then the OS violates the present procedure and resumes the execution of a suspended process. Suppose that the system whose code given in Figure 3.3 is frozen before open() is implemented after access is allowed to get the document/home/Mark/symlink. Then assume an adversary's procedure is chosen for implementation and changes the link to point to etc./passwords. When the initial process is executed again, it is going to start a document (passwords) it did not have consent to perform.

```
If [access("/home/username/symlink", R_OK | W_OK)
!=-1]
{
      // Symbolic link can change here
      f =  fopen("/home/username/symlink", "rw");

      . . .

}
```

Figure 3.3. Code

Operating systems are also vulnerable to installments of malicious extensions and drivers. Kernel extensions, particularly device drivers, now constitute a significant portion of contemporary kernel code foundations (roughly 70 percent in Linux and also a more substantial percent in Windows) (Kadav and Swift 2012). The majority of these extensions are benign and permit the machine to communicate using a growing amount of varied I/O apparatus without the necessity of OS reboot or recompilation. But they pose a danger to system trustworthiness since they run using the maximum degree of privileges and may be malicious or vulnerable. Detection of malicious extensions is quite hard, and most of the suggestions from the literature have not been successful.

Since cloud computing is dependent upon virtualization technologies, vulnerabilities from hypervisors and virtual machine (VM) graphics may also undermine safety. Any mistake or defect in the hypervisor complicated code may endanger the isolation between VMs living in precisely the same server. Cloud computing can be vulnerable to flaws in the system carrying intrusion of VMs one of servers, and another of VM picture and rollback (Hashizume et al. 2013). There are lots of vulnerabilities regarding information that is unique to computing. Data might be found in various countries that have different laws regarding the ownership of data (Ertaul, Singhal, and Gökay 2010). Additionally, data disclosure could occur if data are not eliminated adequately from secondary storage if deleted or moved (Hashizume et al. 2013). In the design layer, precisely like in conventional computing systems, cloud computing is more exposed to hardware Trojans, which present malicious performance in the gate level (Tehranipoor, Salmani, and Zhang 2014).

In the network layer, cloud computing can also be vulnerable to vulnerabilities found in system protocols, usually resulting in a DoS attack like a TCPSYN flooding, in which an adversary sends greater link request packets (SYN packets) than the server can process, and thus makes it inaccessible to legitimate customers (Kurose and Ross 2012).

There are lots of security mechanisms that if applied to the cloud surroundings can help mitigate a number of the vulnerabilities described in the former section. In this section, we share a number of these including mechanisms for information and virtualization safety.

Encryption is often utilized to safeguard the confidentiality of cloud information. It includes the transformation (encoding) of data using mathematical approaches plus a secret key, known as an encryption key. Encrypted data can only be shown to authorized parties utilizing a decryption key.

Encryption prevents an adversary from eavesdropping cloud-sensitive information when it's saved in a data center and transit within the network. Symmetric cryptography uses the same keys to encrypt and decrypt the information, making the algorithms less complicated when compared to their asymmetric counterparts. The level of protection is dependent upon the period of the major. Laura first encrypts the plain text message with Mark's public key, which can be open and accessible to anybody. As an example, Mark will make his public key available at a directory within his business or within a free site. Mark also includes a private key known only to him which differs from his public key. To put it differently, information in plain text that's encrypted using a public key can only be decrypted using the personal correspondent secret. Asymmetric cryptography can be used to fix the challenge of essential supply in symmetric cryptography and as a mechanism to implement digital signatures.

An electronic signature is a method to get a celebrity to guarantee the validity of a message. Digital signatures must achieve non-repudiation; that is, it needs to be hard for a party to invent an electronic name and also to utilize a valid title to get another message.

Asymmetric cryptography is usually used as an automatic signature mechanism in cloud surroundings. In public/private key cryptography, information encrypted with somebody's private key can only be decrypted with that individual's public key. Therefore, if for instance, Mark gets Laura's public key and desires her reliable digital signature in a document sent within the network (a generally untrusted station), he could ask Laura to "signal" or encrypt the information or record together with her private key. If Mark can decrypt the information together with Laura's public key, he can be confident that only Laura could have encrypted the record since she knows her private key. Now let us consider a normal web application in the cloud atmosphere. SSL is a network protocol used to safeguard data between two servers together with encryption. To comprehend the significance of SSL for the security of web applications, think about a situation when you wished to purchase a book from Amazon.

As you are surfing the website, your Internet browser along with the Amazon server are all linked via the normal TCP protocol. Utilizing this kind of link, the information exchanged between your browser (i.e., the things being hunted) along with the Amazon server (i.e., data about Amazon's objects) are not encrypted. Since this market is not encrypted, an adversary that is located on the regional network may leverage network-sniffing applications that inspect the raw information in the system packets exchanged between your browser and Amazon's server. For example, an adversary may learn the consumer of a particular machine is considering novels about Julius Caesar.

Certainly, the consumer should stop an adversary from having the ability to "sniff" her sensitive information like credit card numbers and shipping info. As an example, a user might have typed Amazom.com by error and may be communicating using a bogus browser. So, the consumer would also have to make specific the server carrying the information is Amazon.com.

The SSL protocol accomplishes the demands by employing cryptographic procedures to conceal what is being delivered from one PC to another and from applying identification methods that guarantee that the computer a browser is speaking to is reliable. To put it differently, using SSL to obtain a book from Amazon, the consumer can make confident no adversary will find his/her charge card information and any shared data is exclusively traded together with the actual Amazon.com. As shown in Figure 3.4, as soon as a consumer creates a monetary trade with Amazon.com, the browser and the host set an SSL link under HTTP (https). Notice the way the lock gets obsolete revealing it is a reliable connection. Also, observe that it reads https rather than HTTP. After the user registers the sign-in or login button at e-commerce servers (e.g., Amazon), his browser and the host will set an SSL connection via a "handshake" and after that another identification phase. At the handshake stage, the browser and the server agree on a specific encryption algorithm, and the host sends a certificate to the customer. This certification is a piece of information issued by a trusted certificate authority (CA) that binds a cryptographic public key to a sure thing (e.g., Amazon.com) and is intended to validate if the host is indeed who it is claiming to be.

amazon.com

> ⊗ **There was a problem**
> Enter a valid email or mobile number

Sign In

What is your email (phone for mobile accounts)?

E-mail or mobile number: [_____]

Do you have an Amazon.com password?

○ **I am a new customer.**
(you'll create a password later)

◉ **I am a returning customer, and my password is:**

[_____]

[Sign in using our secure server ⊙]

Forgot your password?

Conditions of Use Privacy Notice
© 1996-2017, Amazon.com, Inc. or its affiliates

Figure 3.4. Amazon user login portal

Hashing is used to create a one-way non-reversible representation of information for safety (Erl, Puttini, and Mahmood 2013; Goodrich and Tamassia 2010; Kurose and Ross 2012). Additionally, once a part of data is hashed there is no way to undo it since there is no "unhash key." Hashing can notify whether information stored at a data center or in transit were endangered (Erl, Puttini, and Mahmood 2013). The message digest is generally more compact than the material itself. If a party should send the message to the network to a different party, it may attach the letter to the news. The receiving party verifies the integrity of this message by applying precisely the same hash function to the signal and also confirming the word is just like the message.

There are lots of functions in the literature covering the safety of VMs operating in the cloud atmosphere. Santos, Gummadi, and Rodrigues (2009) suggested an approach to get a reliable cloud computing system (TCCP) that empowers infrastructure for support (IaaS) solutions like Amazon EC2 to offer a closed-box execution environment. TCCP guarantees private implementation of guest VMs and also permits users to attest to the IaaS supplier and decide whether the service is protected before they launch their own VMs. This strategy includes three modules for the integrity and privacy protection of their sensitive information.

Nowadays, an increasing number of organizations have been embracing public cloud solutions to store their data (e.g., Microsoft Skydrive and Dropbox), in addition to Amazon EC2 and MapReduce Framework, to process there. Research results have shown a continuous growth of cloud adoption where 75 percent of the surveyed in 2013 utilized cloud platforms in contrast to 67 percent in 2012 (Bridge 2013). Using cloud technologies are also useful in compelling data sharing over multiple associations (e.g., government organizations), which can be helpful in many social critical applications, including homeland protection, cybersecurity, illness dispersing control, along with the green market.

But, critical issues of information confidentiality (Cavoukian 2008; Gellman 2009; Jaeger, Lin, and Grimes 2009; Pearson and Charlesworth 2009) interfere with the broad adoption of cloud technologies, mainly public clouds. It is crucial that sensitive information shared and stored from the cloud be firmly secured from unauthorized access. That means information saved in the cloud ought to be shared among different consumers, possibly within distinct organizations, according to access management policies.

When applying access control, it's also essential to protect licensed users' profile information (e.g., user function and place), which may result in inferences about information contents. That is due to advanced access management systems, like the well-known attribute-based access control model (Lin and Squicciarini 2010), demand disclosing enforcement system information about users into the access management. Additionally, data from the cloud might be moved between information centers which might be found in various areas (or even states), in which cloud users do not have a lot of details regarding where their information is processed and stored. Therefore, ensuring privacy during day-to-day surgeries is a challenging undertaking for both cloud support providers (CSPs) and their clients. There is a definite need to create cloud-specific data procuring techniques. The next section first presents a generic cloud information security version and then reviews the state-of-the-art cloud information security methods. The segment concludes with a discussion of another potential cause of information leakage from the cloud.

From the cloud, we observe the following two significant features that impose obstacles in the evolution of information security methods. A cloud service may be given via a string of service providers (Jaeger, Lin, and Grimes 2009). Let's emphasize that the direct service supplier is S and its indirect and direct builders are S1, S2, S(...), and they are to get a person to pick a service supplier. The candidate's support providers' privacy policies will need to be assessed to make certain they conform to customers' privacy preferences. More rigorously, indirect builders' policies might have to be confirmed to fulfill the customers' privacy demands. It's even harder to ensure and apply consumer's privacy requirements throughout multiple parties through the whole service period. Some probable adjustments to the parties included in a cloud support have to be thought of as mentioned in the literature (Gellman 2009): a participating party might want to upgrade its privacy policies, or even a service supplier might want to move its operations jointly with customers' information to somebody else due to the selling of business, a merger, transplant from the authorities, and so on. These events can influence the recent policies agreed to by all parties.

The question is how to effectively and efficiently reflect such a change; the effects of the influence on attaining policy arrangement and policy authorities could be lessened. Specifically, an individual joins the cloud and also confronts a few CSPs, each of them capable of supplying the service that he desires. To be able to discover the service supplier whose privacy policies best match the user's privacy requirements, the consumer's privacy requirements and support suppliers' current privacy policies are fed to the policy standing module collectively. The ranking module assists the user to choose the service supplier with the maximum appropriate privacy policies. Considering that the chosen service provider still might not have policies that exactly match the consumer's requirements, the next step would be to ship their policies into the coverage integration module that will automatically create an integrated policy according to both parties.

The integrated policy will probably be in two formats. One is in a good policy arrangement, that is, a policy written in a particular policy speech. Another is within an executable format (such as a Java JAR file) that is used for the following policy enforcement. Through the procedure, the consumer's data confidentiality will be safeguarded from the executable coverage, even if the executable coverage might additionally travel among builders connected to the direct service provider.

As revealed by the data mentioned above about the security model, the policy enforcement element is essential to the overall safety of the information in the cloud (Cavoukian 2008; Gellman 2009). There have been a few present attempts that aim to deal with this matter. Some strategies (Nabeel et al. 2011; Nabeel, Shang, and Bertino 2013; Shang et al. 2010) use broadcast key management approaches to give access control over the cloud information. This action sort of approaches group information method based on access management policies and reestablishes each category using another key. Users are then granted only the keys to the information items they are permitted to access. These encryption actions need to be carried out in the operator's premises, thereby incurring high communication and computation costs.

As an example, if an individual is revoked, the operator should download the information changed by this change in the cloud, then create a new encryption key, re-encrypt the downloaded information with the new key, then upload the re-encrypted information to his or her cloud. But this strategy is not efficient in managing regular user entries and departures.

To enhance the operation, a few systems use a third party referred to as "proxy" (Pearson and Charlesworth 2009) to run re-encryption in the event of the change of information recipients. But, they do not shield the identifying characteristics of their users.

Another interesting category of work (Sundareswaran et al. 2012) intends to tightly bind information with access management policies to make sure that policies will be mechanically enforced whenever and wherever the data are obtained from. The benefits of utilizing Java techniques are largely twofold. To begin with, JARs supply a lightweight and mobile container for the information in addition to the authority's engine. Secondly, JARs have minimum infrastructure requirements (i.e., a legal Java runtime environment (JRE) running in the remote end) that allow our strategy to be readily embraced. User information items regarding clear policies will be kept in various internal JARs in encoded format together with encrypted log files. The outer JAR includes the authentication module and policy. It's in charge of authenticating entities that wish to get the information, choosing the right internal JAR and implementing the corresponding coverages. The crate is going to be sealed and signed in the structure.

3.3. OTHER POTENTIAL REASONS FOR DATA LEAKAGE FROM THE CLOUD

Apart from enforcing users' privacy policies in their real data file, there is another interesting and fundamental privacy problem brought on by information indexing. Indexes may have a fantastic load of material regarding the information. Since indicators are often assembled after the service supplier gets the user's information and makes the decision to create indicators to improve search functionality, users might not even know about such utilization of the information which likely leaks far more info than that planned by users. The most common strategy for encouraging effective search over spread content is to construct a centered inverted index. The indicator maps every term to some set of files that contain the expression and can be queried from the searcher to acquire a listing of matching documents. Search engines and mediators generally adopt this strategy. As indicated in (Bawa et al. 2009), the strategy can be expanded to encourage access-controlled search by distributing access control policies together with content to the indexing host. The indicator host has to employ these policies for every searcher to filter search results appropriately. Since the indexing host has to be contacted to perform a search fully, searches are tremendously effective.

A centralized index nonetheless exposes content suppliers to anybody who has access to this index structure. This breach of access control might not be tolerable in the cloud, in which assumptions about the trust of this indexing server no longer hold. Further, the compromise of this catalog host by hackers could cause a complete and catastrophic privacy loss. Decentralized indexing is an alternate architecture utilized to identify a specific set of files (or hosts of files) fitting the searcher's query. Access management can be encouraged by making sure the suppliers apply their access policies before providing the files. But, indexes continue to be hosted by untrusted machines over which suppliers have no control. To be able to solve the problems mentioned above, some functions have explored the potential for producing private indicators by relying on predicate-based cryptography (Chang and Mitzenmacher 2004; Yang, Zhong, and Wright 2007).

While noteworthy, these functions lack particular applicability as a result of key management requirements and the computational overhead. Bawa et al. (2009) suggested an intriguing approach to personal indexing by introducing a distributed access control employing protocol. A more recent work (Squicciarini, Sundareswaran, and Lin 2010) addresses the privacy problem from another perspective by enabling the users to obtain better control within the indicators. Specifically, a three-tier data security frame was suggested, which offers powerful, moderate, and low security in line with the information owner's needs. This is accomplished by constructing an identical JAR file as mentioned in the former section. The JAR file encloses both policies and data, and implements the different levels of security as follows:

- **Powerful security:** The service supplier is not permitted to browse the sensitive section of the consumer's document, to negate the probability of communication being conducted in a sensitive part of the record that could result in privacy flows. Users will need to supply sensitive areas regarding their information files. Then the JAR plays the function of choosing which subjects are to be read from the CSPs. The secure fields are just skipped during the continuous reading of this document by identifying the place in which the secure field begins.

- **Moderate security:** This option disables arbitrary access to this information file to avoid successful indexing within the document. The CSP will be enforced to see the material in the following sequence before it can find the information it needs.

- **Low security:** The user specifies undoubtedly from the coverage the use of his information file and the use of indexing. The service supplier is supposed to be trusted and will notify and reconnect with all the users the keywords to be used for indexing purposes.

3.4. PRIVACY AND SECURITY IN MULTICLOUDS

Cloud computing is growing exponentially, whereby there are now hundreds of CSPs of various dimensions (Weinman 2013). A concept of a cloud-of-clouds (also referred to as an intercloud) is suggested and has been studied in recent years (Weinman 2013; Zhu et al. 2012). In a cloud-of-clouds, we distribute information, with a particular degree of redundancy, across several independent clouds managed by different vendors, like the stored data can remain accessible even when a subset of clouds becomes inaccessible. The multicloud environment (Zhu et al. 2012) offers lots of new opportunities and paths to cloud customers. Cloud consumers will be able to leverage not just one cloud provider, but a lot, to fix their diverse requirements and switch providers if a person stops service. To market the multiple clouds, IEEE has initiated the Intercloud Testbed project (Weinman 2013) that helps make interactions among various clouds a reality.

While cloud users may enjoy cheaper data storage and powerful computational capabilities offered by many clouds, customers also face more complicated reliability problems and privacy preservation problems of the outsourced data. More specifically, as it is challenging to get explicit promises on the trustworthiness of each CSP (Owens 2010), cloud consumers are typically advised to adopt searchable encryption methods (Song, Wagner, and Perrig 2000; Kamara and Lauter 2010) to encrypt their outsourced info in a way that the CSPs can immediately search the encrypted data without decryption. Despite many efforts devoted to enhancing the efficiency and security of their searchable encryption, there is little concern for ensuring the reliability of the searchable encrypted information. Though cloud storage provides an on-demand remote backup alternative, it inevitably increases dependability concerns related to having a single point of failure and to possible storage wreck. A perfect multicloud environment should possess the following properties:

- **Reliability:** Given in CSPs, the machine should still operate if t (t < n) CSPs can be found, in which t is a predefined threshold value for your computer.
- **Semantic safety:** The machine should be semantically secure (Curtmola et al. 2006) by fulfilling the following two requirements. First, given the document index and the selection of encoded documents, no adversary could find out any information about the original files except the document spans. Secondly, given a set of trapdoors for a succession of keyword questions, no adversary could find out any information regarding the original documents

except that the access pattern (i.e., the identifiers of those files that contain the query keyword) and the lookup pattern (i.e., if two searches are looking for the same keyword or not).

- **Trapdoor safety:** This necessitates that any information concerning the query keyword—including the search routine—should not be leaked before the multiple CSPs' collaborative searches. The condition holds even if an adversary jeopardizes one CSP.
- **Robustness:** When the protocol successfully finishes, the appropriate files are returned and reconstructed by the users. When the contract aborts, in the collaborative search stage, nothing is returned, and CSPs understand nothing about the document set or the inherent searched keyword.

It is worth noting that not many works consider the issue of simultaneously ensuring searchability, privacy, and reliability on data outsourced to many clouds. Present reliability guarantees solely rely on each CSP's backup option, which however could be a single point of collapse. By way of example, the wreck of Amazon's elastic computing support in 2011 took some favorite social media sites offline for a day and also a single energy department cooperation site was inaccessible for nearly two days. More seriously, this wreck has eternally destroyed many clients' data with serious consequences for some users (Blodget 2011). Recent studies (Chen et al. 2010; Hu et al. 2010) proposed regenerating codes for data reliability in distributed storage like the cloud. Regenerating codes built on the concept of network coding aim at mixing data blocks that are stored in existing storage nodes, and then generating information in a brand new storage node. It is revealed that regenerating codes reduces the data repair/recovery traffic over conventional erasure codes topic to the same fault tolerance level.

One naïve approach to achieve searchability, privacy, and reliability on information outsourced to many clouds is that of trivial replication. In particular, we can replicate the single-user searchable encryption strategy to CSPs. Each CSP stores the same searchable ciphertexts. Thus, even if $n - 1$ CSPs are unavailable, the remote files are still available. But this strategy is not space efficient since it takes a whole lot of capability to conserve the replicas. To reduce redundancy while tolerating CSP failures, another possible approach is to use erasure coding. Specifically, we could use secret sharing methods to encode the files into a set of stocks and distribute the shares to n CSPs so that if a particular number of CSPs are inaccessible, the shares from the rest of the CSPs may be used for reconstructing the original files.

In comparison with the first approach, the second strategy saves storage space by reducing the reliability assurance out of $n - 1$ to $2 - t$.

Besides the downgrading of the reliability guarantee, the second strategy is also more time consuming due to the numerous rounds of communications needed among CSPs to complete the protocol. The STRE (storage and retrieval mechanism) empowers cloud users to disperse and search their encrypted data in CSPs living in multiple clouds while obtaining reliability. The STRE mechanism follows a similar spirit to the second naïve approach and proposes more efficient secret sharing-based protocols. Moreover, the STRE mechanism also has better protection on the consumer's search pattern. Especially, many works (Curtmola et al. 2006; Kamara, Papamanthou, and Roeder 2012) on searchable encryption would completely disclose the consumer's search pattern which indicates whether two hunts are for the same query keyword or not. From the STRE mechanism, this type of pattern escape risk is decreased because the search is conducted on a dispersed basis and the search routine will be revealed only if higher than t CSPs collude.

An overview of the STRE mechanism is given below. The STRE mechanism is composed of three significant phases: the setup phase, the storage phase, and the recovery phase. During the setup phase, a master secret key is generated from a security parameter and delegated to the cloud user. During the storage period, the user requires a group of input files and the master secret key and creates a set of file shares and a file index. The file shares and document indicator are uploaded to the corresponding CSP. The recovery phase is to search the files containing a particular keyword.

The user generates a set of trapdoor shares based on the query keyword and his or her master key. The trapdoor discussion is delivered to the various CSPs—the consumer. Last, the user reconstructs and decrypts the results and gets the files that are clear, each of which contains the query keyword.

3.5. CLOUD ACCOUNTABILITY

One of the primary motives underlying cloud computing methods is the chance to outsource complicated computation and to save large quantities of information. But to this date, customers have few, if any, specialized techniques to check resource consumption and data storage status, as soon as they are "sent" to the cloud providers. Cloud suppliers do not allow users to observe their inner workings, and consumers have no reliable information about their information whereabouts or the status of their actual computation. While encryption can guarantee the confidentiality of outsourced data, and access control may enhance these guarantees by controlling who is accessing what percentage of data (or, more generally, resources), ensuring the integrity and confirming how much data is being used is hard. To deal with these issues, accountability is an important security condition in cloud technologies. Accountability aims at supplying a detective, rather than a preventive remedy to cloud users (Ko et al. 2011).

The goal is not to protect data privacy or control resource use, but instead to confirm who has got access to resources, and also how. Based on Ruebsamen and Reich (Ruebsamen and Reich. 2013), cloud liability can help "make data processing from the cloud more transparent," so that "seized data-lifecycle events can be matched against policies in Tests and thereby show the customer, that his information is handled appropriately." Unlike privacy protection technology, which is built on the hide-it-or-lose-it perspective, accountability focuses on keeping the information usage transparent and trackable.

Traditional liability methods focus on information collection and postmortem analysis, and third-party audits. Usually, an accountability system will include data collection, through log group and event monitoring, followed by auditing and evaluation of the accumulated evidence to detect potential anomalies or to check actual data lineage. However, as stated by Ko et al. (2011), cloud computing's guarantee of elasticity empowered by virtualization introduces a few new complexities in accountability, associated with the ability of monitoring and processing multiple virtual and physical resources, connected in an incredibly dynamic fashion. Further, the log collection becomes a challenging task in itself, as a result of potentially limited trust assumed at distant nodes, which may not be dependable enough to collect the evidence required for current liability.

Though the present industry practice relies on contractual and regulatory arrangements between cloud and client suppliers to ensure data and resource accountability (Pearson 2011), researchers have investigated ways to overcome the above challenges via technical means. A frequent approach is to rely on logs produced as part of the computation and storage procedure, possibly augmented with ad-hoc information necessary to monitor access and other activities against the report. Recent work has suggested doing this by using digital proof bags to address interoperability and evidence ethics, while further metadata may be utilized to facilitate evidence processing (Ruebsamen and Reich 2013). Others have suggested using agents to promote distributed data collection and provide a more vital infrastructure (Gellman 2009; Sundareswaran, Squicciarini, and Lin 2012).

Cloud provenance concentrates on recording ownership and processing history of information objects, and it is considered a significant factor in the success of data forensics in cloud computing (Asghar et al. 2011; Lu et al. 2010). In particular, researchers have emphasized that provenance can be a means to derive the so-called chain of custody, which should portray how the data were gathered, examined, and maintained. This is particularly critical for cloud forensics, that is, in the event of a legal dispute, to ensure that provenance information is admissible as proof in court. Among existing proposals, a recent project on provenance depends on the idea of provable data ownership (PDP) (Gellman 2009), which mainly builds cryptographic proofs of data possession which could be verified at the customer end. The very same vulnerabilities, threats, and strikes that affect traditional computing are a risk to cloud computing, with added threats coming from using virtualized resources and hypervisors. This chapter also discussed countermeasures for threats at many layers of abstraction. Later, this chapter addressed privacy and safety in cloud-storage solutions and multiclouds, and cloud liability.

The most significant research challenge in cloud safety is the way that cloud suppliers can assure a degree of security to cloud clients. Cloud customers do not have any choice but to trust their cloud providers, and they usually have no assurances on the level of safety being supplied.

REFERENCES

Asghar, M.R., M. Ion, G. Russello, and B. Crispo. 2011. Securing Data Provenance in the Cloud. *Proceedings of the IFIP WG 11.4 International Conference on Open Problems in Network Security (iNetSec)*, June 9, Lucerne, Switzerland.

Bawa, M., R.J. Bayardo, R. Agrawal, and J. Vaidya. 2009. "Privacy-Preserving Indexing of Documents on the Network." *Very Large Data Base Journal* 18, no. 4, pp. 837–56.

Bishop, M. 2003. *Computer Security: Art and Science*. Boston, MA: Addison Wesley.

Blodget, H. 2011. "Amazon's Cloud Crash Disaster Permanently Destroyed Many Customers."

Bridge, N. 2013. "2013 Future of Cloud Computing Survey Reveals Business Driving Cloud Adoption in Everything as a Service Era." https://nblp.northbridge .com/weblp

Cavoukian, A. 2008. "Privacy in the Clouds." *Identity in the Information Society* 1, no. 1, pp. 89–108.

Chang, Y.-C., and M. Mitzenmacher. 2004. "Privacy Preserving Keyword Searches on Remote Encrypted Data."

Chen, B., R. Curtmola, G. Ateniese, and R. Burns. 2010. Remote Data Checking for Network Coding-Based Distributed Storage Systems. *Proceedings of 2010 ACM Workshop on Cloud Computing Security*, October 8, pp. 31–42, Chicago, IL.

Curtmola, R., J.A. Garay, S. Kamara, and R. Ostrovsky. 2006. Searchable Symmetric Encryption: Improved Definitions and Efficient Constructions. *Proceedings of the 13th ACM Conference on Computer and Communications Security (CCS)*, October 30 to November 3, pp. 79–88, Alexandria, VA.

Erl, T., R. Puttini, and Z. Mahmood. 2013. *Cloud Computing: Concepts, Technology & Architecture.* Upper Saddle River, NJ: Prentice Hall.

Ertaul, L., S. Singhal, and S. Gökay. 2010. Security Challenges in Cloud Computing. *Proceedings of the International Conference on Security and Management (SAM),* July 12–15, pp. 36–42, Las Vegas, NV.

Gellman, R. 2009. "Privacy in the Clouds: Risks to Privacy and Confidentiality from Cloud Computing," *World Privacy Forum.*

Goodrich, M., and R. Tamassia. 2010. *Introduction to Computer Security.* Boston, MA: Pearson,

Grobauer, B., T. Walloschek, and E. Stocker. 2011. "Understanding Cloud Computing Vulnerabilities." *IEEE Security & Privacy* 9, no. 2, pp. 50–57.

Hashizume, K., D.G. Rosado, E. Fernández-Medina, and E.B. Fernandez. 2013. "An Analysis of Security Issues for Cloud Computing." *Journal of Internet Services and Applications* 4, p. 5.

Hu, Y., Y. Xu, X. Wang, C. Zhan, and P. Li. 2010. "Cooperative Recovery of Distributed Storage Systems from Multiple Losses with Network Coding." *IEEE Journal on Selected Areas in Communications* 28, pp. 268–76.

Jaeger, P.T., J. Lin, and J.M. Grimes. 2009. "Cloud Computing and Information Policy: Computing in a Policy Cloud?" *Journal of Information Technology and Politics* 5, no. 3, pp. 269–83.

Kadav, A., and M.M. Swift. 2012. Understanding Modern Device Drivers. *Proceedings of the 17th International Conference on Architectural Support for Programming Languages and Operating Systems (ASPLOS),* March 3–7, London, England.

Kamara, S., and K. Lauter. 2010. "Cryptographic Cloud Storage, Financial Cryptography and Data Security." *Ser. Lecture Notes in Computer Science* 6054, pp. 136–49.

Kamara, S., C. Papamanthou, and T. Roeder. 2012. Dynamic Searchable Symmetric Encryption. *Proceedings of 2012 ACM Conference on Computer and Communications Security,* October 16–18, pp. 965–76, Raleigh, NC.

Ko, R.K.L., P. Jagadpramana, M. Mowbray, S. Pearson, M. Kirchberg, Q. Liang, and B.S. Lee. 2011. TrustCloud: A Framework for Accountability and Trust in Cloud Computing. *Proceedings of 2011 IEEE World Congress on Services,* July 4–9, Washington, DC.

Kurose, J., and K. Ross. 2012. *Computer Networking: A TopDown Approach.* London, England: Pearson.

Lhee, K.-S., and S.J. Chapin. 2003. "Buffer Overflow and Format String Overflow Vulnerabilities." *Software—Practice and Experience* 33, no. 5, pp. 423–60.

Lin, D., and A. Squicciarini. 2010. Data Protection Models for Service Provisioning in the Cloud. *Proceedings of the 15th ACM Symposium on Access Control Models and Technologies,* June 9–11, pp. 183–192, Pittsburgh, PA.

Lu, R., X. Lin, X. Liang, and X. Shen. 2010. Secure Provenance: The Essential of Bread and Butter of Data Forensics in Cloud Computing. *Proceedings of the 5th ACM Symposium on Information, Computer and Communications Security (ASIACCS),* April 13–16, pp. 282–92, Beijing, China.

Nabeel, M., E. Bertino, M. Kantarcioglu, and B. Thuraisingham. 2011. Towards Privacy Preserving Access Control in the Cloud. *Proceedings of the 7th International Conference on Collaborative Computing: Networking, Applications and Worksharing (Collaborate Com)*, October 15–18, pp. 172–180, Orlando, FL.

Nabeel, M., N. Shang, and E. Bertino. 2013. "Privacy Preserving Policy-Based Content Sharing in Public Clouds." *IEEE Transaction on Knowledge and Data Engineering* 25, no. 11, pp. 2602–14.

Owens, D. 2010. "Securing Elasticity in the Cloud." *Communications of the ACM* 53, pp. 46–51.

Pearson, S. 2011. "Toward Accountability in the Cloud." *IEEE Internet Computing* 4, pp. 64–69.

Pearson, S., and A. Charlesworth. 2009. "Accountability as a Way Forward for Privacy Protection in the Cloud," *Hewlett-Packard Development Company* (HPL-2009-178).

Ruebsamen, T., and C. Reich. 2013. Supporting Cloud Accountability by Collecting Evidence Using Audit Agents. *Proceedings of 2013 IEEE 5th International Conference on Cloud Computing Technology and Science (CloudCom)*. Vol. 1, December 2–5, Bristol, England.

Santos, N., K. Gummadi, and R. Rodrigues. 2009. Towards Trusted Cloud Computing. *Proceedings of the 2009 Conference on Hot Topics in Cloud Computing*, June 14–19, San Diego, CA.

Shang, N., M. Nabeel, F. Paci, and E. Bertino. 2010. A Privacy-Preserving Approach to Policy-Based Content Dissemination. *Proceedings of IEEE 26th International Conference on Data Engineering (ICDE)*, March 1–6, pp. 944–55, Long Beach, CA.

Song, D.X., D. Wagner, and A. Perrig. 2000. Practical Techniques for Searches on Encrypted Data. *Proceedings of 2000 IEEE Symposium on Security and Privacy*, May 14–17, pp. 44–55, Berkeley, CA.

Squicciarini, A., S. Sundareswaran, and D. Lin. 2010. Preventing Information Leakage from Indexing in the Cloud. *Proceedings of 2010 IEEE International Conference on Cloud Computing*, July 5-10, Miami, FL.

Stallings, W., and L. Brown. 2012. *Computer Security Principles and Practice*. Harlow, England: Pearson.

Su, Z., and G. Wassermann. 2006. The Essence of Command Injection Attacks in Web Applications. *ACM SIGPLAN-SIGACT Symposium on Principles of Programming (POPL)*, January 11–13, pp. 372–382, Charleston, SC.

Sundareswaran, S., A. Squicciarini, D. Lin, and S. Huang. 2012. "Ensuring Distributed Accountability for Data Sharing in the Cloud." *IEEE Transactions on Dependable and Secure Computing (TDSC)* 9, no. 4, pp. 556–68.

Tehranipoor, M., H. Salmani, and X. Zhang. 2014. *Integrated Circuit Authentication—Hardware Trojans and Counterfeit Detection*. Springer, New York, NY.

Vulnerabilities. *International Conference on Software Engineering (ICSE)*, May 10–18, pp. 171–180, Leipzig, Germany.

Weinman, J. 2013. "Will Multiple Clouds Evolve into the Intercloud?" https://www.wired.com/insights/2013/10/will-multiple-clouds-evolve-into-the-intercloud/

Yang, Z., S. Zhong, and N. Wright. 2007. Towards PrivacyPreserving Model Selection. *Proceedings of the 1st ACM SIGKDD International Conference on Privacy, Security, and Trust in KDD (PinKDD)*, August 12, pp. 138–152, San Jose, CA.

Zhu, Y., H. Hu, G.-J. Ahn, and M. Yu. 2012. "Cooperative Provable Data Possession for Integrity Verification in Multicloud Storage." *IEEE Transactions on Parallel Distributed Systems* 23, no. 12, pp. 2231–44.

CHAPTER 4

CLOUD COMPUTING ARCHITECTURE

From the first days of computing, mainframe computers controlled the age of information processing before the dawn of personal computers (PCs). Mainframe and minicomputers were placed in the information centers. Computing art of mainframe computers has been obtained using dumb terminals connected to mainframe computers through dial-up modems and committed network connections.

The appearance of PCs introduced the computing paradigm into local area networks (LANs), thereby minimizing the part of mainframe and minicomputers. In the last 10 years, PC hardware has got processing capacities for mainframes, as well as the fact that media hardware and software is capable of supplying more robust and dependable connectivity.

The elements of cloud computing structure are all software and hardware that is required for its shipping of cloud computing solutions. What is more, these elements of a cloud computing structure are coordinated into deploying cloud or platforms customers, backend platforms such as servers and storage devices, along with a route connecting the backend of one system into the backend of the other system to get the cloud-based solutions as exemplified in Figure 4.1.

This route is the system, which is either a public (Internet) or a personal network. The function of this network is to provide services.

Cloud computing suppliers provide cloud computing solutions, so that cloud clients can benefit from the advantages of cloud computing and help them reach their targets. Cloud suppliers offer you various providers, and the cloud hosting providers might also be set up and introduced through various procedures. Cloud suppliers allocate physical tools, relevant sources, or both to their clients (a few examples of sources are processing memory, memory, network bandwidth, virtual machines, applications, etc.); however, generally cloud computing solutions have the common attributes as illustrated in Figure 4.1.

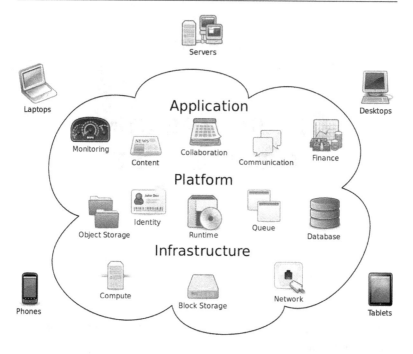

Figure 4.1. Cloud computing structure

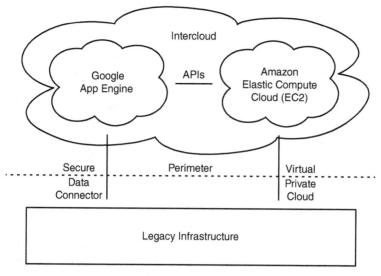

Virtual Private Cloud (VPC)

Figure 4.2. Cloud computing solution's features

Cloud resources and services can be retrieved readily by clients and users via a network like web services or tools on demand: Clients can use resources according to their requirements at any time and in any place. Highly scalable tools and support capabilities can be reached automatically. Services are quantified: the use of their allocated resources and solutions (for example, processing, storage, memory, etc.) may be controlled, measured, managed, and documented so both clients and suppliers may have a clear view within the wants and consumption of their resources.

Cloud customers are of many types, but generally, a cloud customer is a computing system that uses cloud solutions (Hofer and Howanitz 2009). Cloud customers are described either in the context of hardware or applications; in the sections below, hardware and applications customer types will be analyzed in a few cases.

4.1. HARDWARE CUSTOMERS

The expression "hardware customers" refers to cloud customers who are distinguished based on hardware features of computing systems.

Hardware customers are of three kinds, as shown in Figure 4.3.

Figure 4.3. Hardware customers. Thick clients, lean customers, smartphones, hardware customers

4.1.1. THICK CLIENTS

Thick clients refer to computing systems that perform substantial information processing from the client/server version. Thick clients have a lot of ports, internal memory, input and output devices like PCs. With thick clients, there is no need for continuous communication between clients and servers. Nearly all available cloud solutions are created for thin clients, including Microsoft LiveMesh along with the Elastic Compute Cloud (EC2).

4.1.2. THIN CLIENTS

A thin client is generally a terminal that is not meant for significant processing and renders the processing responsibilities of bulky information to a host. A thin client is a network computer without a hard disk that functions as broadcasts communicating with a host. Thin client typical programs have been in areas in which the end user has particular activities for which the machine is utilized, like schools, authorities, manufacturing plants, and so forth.

4.1.3. SMARTPHONES

Within the past 10 years, we have noticed the processing capacity of mobile devices based on iOS and Android operating systems has attained the same level of support as notebooks and desktop PCs. Such cellular devices support both Wi-Fi and LTE connectivity, so a roaming customer can get any services that are cloud-based. Safety is a vital issue once the roaming customer accomplishes financial portfolio management, electronic banking transactions, and social media. In forthcoming years, mobile devices will start to replace PCs as the display size on the apparatus gets more substantial, thus enabling a complete page view.

4.1.4. SOFTWARE CUSTOMERS

Computer software customers refer to cloud customers who are distinguished according to applications functionality; for instance, some cloud software demand Internet connectivity while the program is functioning, whereas additional cloud software can operate offline but with limited purposes. Software customers are of three kinds as shown in Figure 4.4.

4.1.5. THICK OR THIN . . . OR SMART?

A thin client machine is going to communicate with a central processing server, meaning there is not much hardware and software installed on the user's machine. Occasionally, thin may be defined as simply not needing the software or operating system installed on the user machine. This permits all end users' systems to be centrally managed and software set up on a central server location as opposed to being set up on each individual system. Thin clients are best suited to surroundings where the exact same information will be accessed by the clients, which makes it a better solution for public environments. Because of this, thin clients are often deployed in airports and resorts, where installing software in all systems would not make sense. It would be a huge headache for IT to both deploy and maintain. When compared with the feature-rich desktop PCs, thin clients often

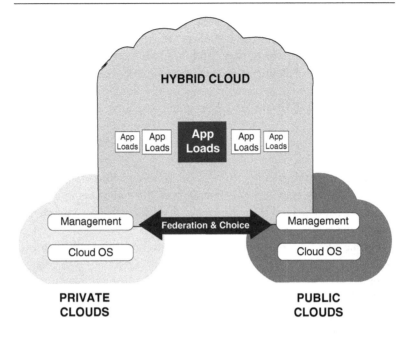

Figure 4.4. Thick or Thin customers, web software customers (or occasionally thin customers), Bright customers

tend to look somewhat primitive and obsolete. Because most thin clients run on very little hardware, it is impossible to incorporate rich graphical user interfaces. All that the customer needs are an input device (keyboard) and a seeing device (display). Some may not require a mouse.

By comparison, a thick client provides users with more attributes, images, and choices making the applications more customizable. Unlike thin clients, thick clients do not rely upon a central processing host because the processing is performed locally on the user system, and the server is obtained mostly for storage purposes. For that reason, heavy clients frequently are not suited for public surroundings. To maintain a heavy client, all systems for software installation and updates have to be maintained, rather than just keeping the software on the server. Additionally, heavy customers often require operating certain applications, again introducing more limitations and work for deployment.

Over the past couple of years, the general drift is to move toward smart clients, also called wealthy customers. The trend is a movement from conventional client/server architecture to a model that is contemporary.

More like a thick client vs. a thin client, smart clients are Internet-connected apparatus that allows a user's local applications to socialize with server-based programs by using web services. For instance, a wise client running a word processing application might interface with a remote database online so as to collect data from the database to be used in the word processing document. Smart clients support offline operations. In other words, they could use data even if they are not on the Internet (which distinguishes them from browser-based applications, which do not work when the unit is not on the web). Smart client software has the capability to be deployed and upgraded in real time over the system from a dedicated server. They support multiple languages and platforms since they are built on web services, and can operate on almost any device that has Internet connectivity, including desktops, workstations, notebooks, tablet PCs, PDAs, and mobile phones. Smart clients offer rich graphical user interfaces (GUIs), and overall development and maintenance costs are higher than, for instance, thin clients. On the downside, smart clients require customers to install or set up a runtime library—routines that are bound to the program during execution. Smart clients are most frequently contrasted with web browser clients (or browser-based applications).

4.1.6. THIN OR WEB-APPLICATIONS CUSTOMERS

All attributes typically found on the desktop PC, including software, sensitive information, memory, and so on, are saved back in the data center when using a thin client. A thin client running Remote Desktop Protocols (RDP), such as Citrix ICA and Windows Terminal Services, and/or virtualization software, accesses hard drives from the information center stored on servers, blades, and such items. Thin clients, software solutions, and backend hardware make up thin client computing, a digital desktop computing version. Thin clients serve as PC replacement technology to help customers immediately access any virtual desktop or virtualized application. Thin clients provide businesses a cost-effective approach to create a virtual desktop infrastructure (VDI). Thin clients are used in a variety of industries and enterprises worldwide that have different prerequisites but share common objectives. The cost, security, manageability, and scalability benefits of thin clients are all reasons that IT personnel are researching—and switching—to thin clients.

4.1.7. SMART CUSTOMERS

Smart customers have software that not only allows them to keep the majority of their information on the World Wide Web, but they also benefit from the processing power and other sources of a PC to make sure of a better user experience. There are three kinds of cloud customers' applications use:

1. Web-based customers: Where resources are obtained via an Internet browser.
2. Client software: The cloud tools are obtained through software.
3. Programs with cloud extensions: Several desktop programs have discretionary extensions to the cloud.

Cloud suppliers have the infrastructure needed to give cloud solutions for clients most common storage solutions and applications. Cloud suppliers utilize various platforms and technologies to ensure appropriate service delivery—illustrations of these platforms are cloud servers and storage. Cloud storage offers storage solutions, while cloud servers operate clients' programs.

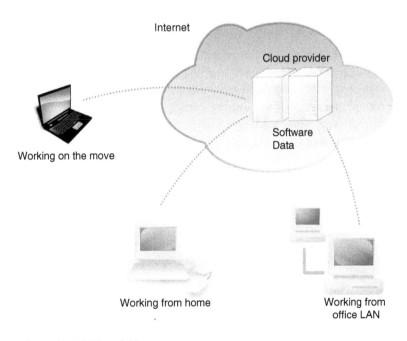

Figure 4.5. Thick and thin customers

Cloud storage is a version of storing electronic information in pools that are reasonable; the storage can span some servers frequently in numerous places. The physical environment is generally handled and owned by a hosting firm. Storage providers are accountable for the accessibility and availability of their information, and also for keeping the physical surroundings running and protected. Cloud storage relies on highly virtualized infrastructure and generally identifies some hosted item storage assistance. However, the term has broadened to include different kinds of information storage which are currently available as a support, such as storage.

Companies only need to cover the actual storage that they use, but that does not automatically suggest that cloud storage is not as costly.

Storage upkeep tasks are offloaded to support suppliers. Cloud-storage supply users have instant access to a wide selection of resources. Cloud storage may be utilized as a natural catastrophe proof backup.

Security concerns and lack of information: Performance for outsourced storage is dependent upon cost, performance, reliability, and quality of service (QoS) provided by telecommunication suppliers due to their WAN connections over aluminum or fiber-based circuits. Websites that allow file sharing might enable piracy and copyright infringement.

A cloud host is a reasonable server that is hosted via a cloud computing system across the people (Internet) or personal network. Cloud servers give the same quality of support as a local server even if the service is obtained remotely by a cloud supplier. A cloud server may be described as infrastructure for support (IaaS) from the cloud support module.

In certain respects, cloud servers operate in exactly the same way as servers; however, the functions they supply can be extremely different. When selecting cloud hosting, customers are leasing virtual server space instead of leasing or buying physical servers, which is usually covered by the hour, based on the capability required at any specific moment.

Virtual machines are software implementations of a system (for instance, a computer) and also have their own operating system (OS) and implement applications like physical machines. In a cloud surrounding, modern physical hardware might be divided into a limited number of virtual machines, which can be assigned to a client. This also contributes to a more efficient consumption of computing tools. Different kinds of digital machine OSs may coexist on precisely the same hardware, but digital segregation is needed to coordinate the performance of this OS. In this delivery model, the machine is distributed into a few logical servers, every logical server using its different OS, user interfaces, and software, though they share the identical physical server.

Cloud computing suppliers provide their services based on three basic models (Hayes 2008) as shown in Figure 4.6. Listed below are the three kinds of cloud computing:

- Software as a service, SaaS, is also known as "on-demand software." Users of SaaS, rather than buying different software, hire the software at regular intervals, and use it via an online browser.

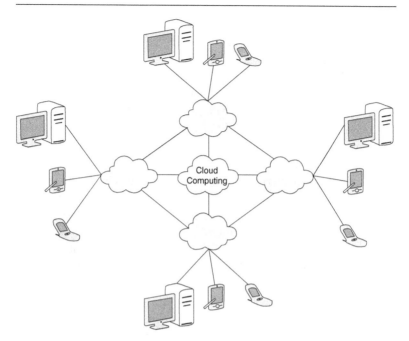

Figure 4.6. Cloud computing suppliers provide their services based on three basic models

The assortment of software provided by SaaS is very broad. The software-as-a-service type of cloud computing grows quite quickly. The largest market for software-as-a-service is customer relationship management.

• PaaS provides computer platforms for users of cloud computing. It is also the link between both the other services supplied by cloud computing; SaaS and IaaS.

A standard computer requires a computer platform which includes hardware and architecture, along with a frame of applications. Such a stage is the cornerstone of the collaboration of hardware and applications, which includes the OS, languages, and architecture. When it comes to cloud computing, in the absence of a real computer, it is platform as a service that provides users with all that is required to write a computing system. A few of the facilities that PaaS provides include hosting, implementation, test and program development, and application design. Additionally, cloud service providers offering PaaS comprise a set of qualities to design, test, implement, manage, and run programs. These facilities may be used by both personal and business clients, by subscribing into one package with all the features offered.

The platform-as-a-service (PaaS) version is a level over the software-as-a-service setup and provides hardware, network, and OS support so that a customer can design his or her own applications. To be able to meet the requirements of applications such as scalability and manageability, the customer must opt for a predefined combination of OS and application servers from PaaS sellers, for example, at any phase of the process to develop, test, and ultimately host their sites, web developers can utilize respective PaaS environments.

- IaaS is the next type of computing across the cloud. The same as PaaS and SaaS, which are different software and hardware devices provided on a cloud platform, while IaaS gives a virtualized platform. The process of hardware virtualization shows the users only the abstract computing platform instead of the physical platform. Such virtualization leads to the creation of a so-called "virtual machine monitor" or even "hypervisor," that's the creation of this next part of the cloud computing system, that is, Interface as a Service. Infrastructure available to customers of IaaS includes software, servers, network devices, and data center space. The fee incurred by customers' cloud service providers typically depend on the amount of service used by the consumer and is therefore not set. But, there is a minimum charge the consumer will have to pay depending on the number of amenities a user has subscribed to.

IaaS is a basic computing and storage area provided by a standardized service over the network. This version has made the workload easier by consolidating and providing data center space, storage systems, network servers, devices, and so on. Additionally, the client can develop and install his or her own OSs, applications, and software.

There are various advantages in utilizing cloud computer technology. However, any type of cloud service has its own set of advantages and pitfalls. In order to make the right decision, it is very important that users carefully weigh the advantages and disadvantages.

IaaS is thought of as the simplest cloud support model, and as stated by the IETF (Internet technology task force), suppliers of IaaS offer computers—physical or (more commonly) virtual machines—as well as other resources. Within an IaaS version, tools such as host hardware, software, servers, storage, and other infrastructure elements can be given to customers.

Cloud suppliers that provide IaaS provide on-demand and extremely scalable tools, making IaaS acceptable for workloads that are temporary, experimental, or change suddenly. Furthermore, IaaS can be a fantastic solution for some organizations with no funds to invest in hardware or other tools, or businesses that are experiencing rapid expansion where climbing hardware could be hard.

Many businesses nowadays prefer to outsource servers, applications, data centers, and so forth as opposed to buying the tools. Here they can find a full on-demand support. While IaaS suppliers can provide substantial benefits for some businesses and associations, there are many instances where its constraints could be debatable such as in companies where high performance is essential, or wherever regulatory compliance prevents the outsourcing of information processing or storage.

From the PaaS version, cloud suppliers provide computing platforms that generally incorporate an OS, programming language implementation environment, database, and a web server. Some PaaS suppliers give customers scalable tools, in which the underlying storage and computer resources scale automatically in line with the applications' requirements and so the cloud customer does not need to allocate funds manually. PaaS providers usually offer you a computing platform that permits the creation of web applications speedily and effectively, which enables clients to avoid the complexity of getting and keeping the infrastructure and software needed for the endeavor. PaaS is much like SaaS except that instead of providing applications over the network, the platform for the production of applications is delivered across the Internet. PaaS fundamental attributes usually contain the following:

- Many PaaS platforms provide multitenant architectures where concurrent, and several users use the exact same improvement program.
- Some PaaS platforms encourage team cooperation development.
- Most PaaS platforms provide tools to take care of billing and subscription control.

PaaS is regarded as most useful in circumstances where multiple programmers are working on a development project or at which other outside parties will need to socialize with the development endeavor. Furthermore, PaaS can also be useful where programmers mean to automate testing and installation services.

There are some scenarios where PaaS might not be the ideal alternative; for instance, situations in which a proprietary speech could affect or interfere moves to a different supplier afterwards, or in which the functioning of the program involves customizing the underlying applications and hardware. Some examples of the most Frequent PaaS suppliers are Microsoft Azure Services, Google App Engine, as well as the Force.com platform.

SaaS is the ideal platform for business applications that were intended for specific functions, where cloud suppliers handle the platforms and infrastructure which runs the software.

SaaS has two different modes:

- **Single tenant SaaS architecture:** While there is absolutely no system that is one hundred percent secure, single tenant surroundings more easily allow for greater safety as every client's data is completely separate from any others. The chance that one customer will accidentally access the data (like in a multitenant environment) is basically eliminated.
- **Single renter architectures:** These are commonly regarded as more reliable because the performance of one customer's software instance is not affected by the operation of some other customers.

In one renter environment, you need more control over backups and recovery as a single system is backed up to a dedicated portion of a SaaS server. On the other hand, in a multitenancy environment, this process is much more elaborate to the point that it is not always readily available for users.

For enterprises that may eventually wish to move to self-hosted surroundings, by using a single tenancy the procedure becomes less complex.

In one tenancy, you have full control over the environment. That means the platform offers a great deal more flexibility in terms of customization. And also more control over updates and upgrades.

- **Multitenant SaaS Architecture:** Monetary benefits of a multitenant operation is that the per user price is reduced because all resources are shared. If you are searching for a solution that produces the most financial sense, a multitenancy could be exactly what you are after. Since every one of the resources is shared, multitenancies function at maximum resource usage, which makes for optimum efficiency. The system is a continuously moving environment where resources are being concurrently accessed. SaaS platforms offering multitenant environments are usually sticklers for offering top-notch customer service. That is because they have a higher volume of consumers and need to make sure each has a good experience.

    Updates applied to the system affect all clients and as such system updates and update maintenance are often handled by the SaaS company, and not the individual client. As a result of this, multitenancies generally require less upkeep.

The distinction between multi-tenancy and multi-enterprise is worth noting as they are two very different theories but maybe easy to confuse.

Multi-enterprise, also referred to as multiple-enterprise small business systems are B2B ecosystems that enable a couple of parties to collaborate on an activity. On the other hand, a multitenant environment identifies a seller related term describing the way the software solution is handled.

Multitenant architectures is the industry standard for enterprise SaaS applications but that does not mean developers should eschew the notion of operating one tenant environment instead. Each has its very best use case. When deciding which is right for you, it's important to think about exactly what you need to accomplish. If you think about what is going to provide a development environment similar to your present one, in some cases, you may make a case for single tenant usage. As an example, if you would like total control over the environment and upkeep, you might choose to invest in a single tenant ecosystem. But single renter infrastructures might be more awkward and bulky for companies looking for the very seamless digital transformation. In terms of SaaS startups, there is barely one out there today that is operating in a single tenancy. But for companies hoping to transition from a controlled server environment to any self-hosted one, single tenancy is ideal.

There are five primary architectural deployments of this cloud computing solution for cloud customers, as exemplified in Figure 4.7:

- Personal
- Virtual personal
- Hybrid
- Community
- Public

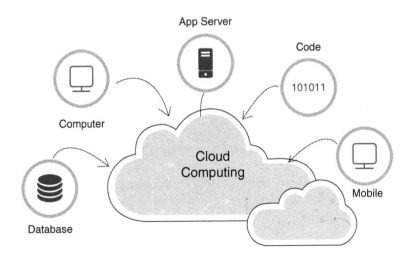

Figure 4.7. Cloud setup version

Figure 4.8 illustrates the installation of the cloud model:

- Highly scalable tools since cloud tools are available on need
- High access to cloud solutions and assets
- Reduces price
- Adaptive services
- Location-independent accessibility to solutions

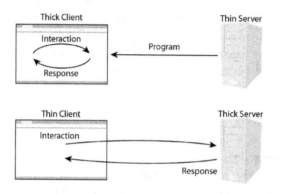

Figure 4.8. Illustrates the installation of the cloud model

4.1.8. PERSONAL CLOUD

This kind of deployment essentially gives organizations the capability to make a remote data center. This model often gives the maximum degree of control from a safety standpoint. A personal cloud is a sort of cloud computing structure that provides services like the public cloud such as scalability and flexibility; however, unlike people clouds, which provide services to numerous organizations, a personal cloud is committed to one company as shown in Figure 4.9. Unlike cloud-storage services like DropBox and Google Drive, a private cloud is possessed and controlled by an individual: instead of leasing space on the Internet, an individual purchases a storage method and links it to the web. Not long ago, preparing a personal cloud-storage system would have basically required the individual to build a server. But now, thanks to consumer-friendly systems from D-Link, Western Digital, and Seagate, among others, the individual needs to do little more than plug in the device.

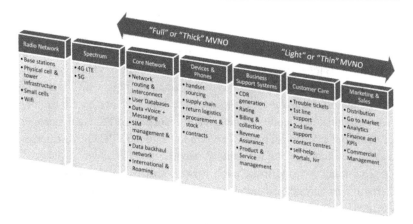

Figure 4.9. Personal cloud is committed to one company

4.1.9. VIRTUAL PRIVATE CLOUD

A Virtual Private Cloud includes on-demand shared computing tools that could be allocated to clients in cloud surroundings as exemplified in Figure 4.10. A virtual private cloud (VPC) is a personal cloud found inside a public cloud that permits you to experience the benefits of a virtualized network while utilizing people cloud resources. A VPC isolates your

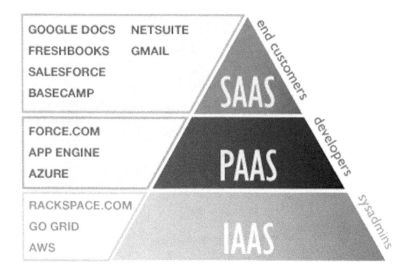

Figure 4.10. Virtual private cloud

information from that of other businesses—both in transit and at the cloud provider's network—helping to create a more secure environment. A VPC connects to remote networks via a virtual private network (VPN) connection. A VPC is ideal for companies seeking high levels of security, privacy, and management, such as health care and financial organizations dealing with regulatory compliance. Businesses also find VPC perfect for running mission-critical applications. One usually manages a VPC via a managed service supplier's control panel. This window into the VPC allows a person to easily see and make adjustments as needed.

This kind of cloud installation version provides a cloud computing alternative to a restricted number of businesses which are handled and procured commonly by all of the participating parties or a third-party managed service supplier as shown in Figure 4.11. Ordinarily, this kind of deployment incorporates specific organizations with similar policies or requirements which may benefit from precisely the same infrastructure, or associations that are focusing on joint projects, researches, or software

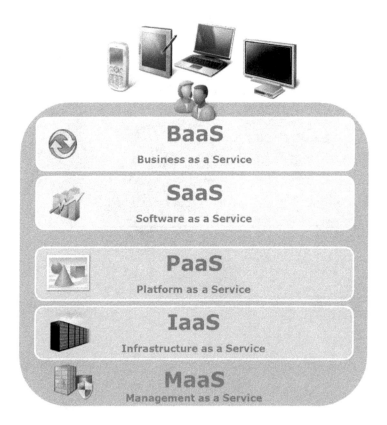

Figure 4.11. Third-party managed service supplier

that demand a central computing center. Community clouds could be regarded as a hybrid design of personal clouds.

The hybrid model is made up of a blend of private and public cloud tools, where the private and public cloud infrastructures operate independently and typically speak over an encrypted link as shown in Figure 4.12. It is necessary to see that the private and public clouds are different and separate components. Typically, organizations store critical or significant data in the personal cloud, and along with the public cloud they may use the private cloud to receive computational tools that applications rely upon, which enhances safety and reduces the information vulnerability to an accepted minimal. Hybrid clouds possess many advantages and deliver many options, since this deployment version is acceptable for producing a backup when failover scenarios happen, or when there are equilibrium heavy workloads, and can be far more cost-effective than personal clouds and other benefits based on the example. Figure 4.12 presents the type of cloud installation version.

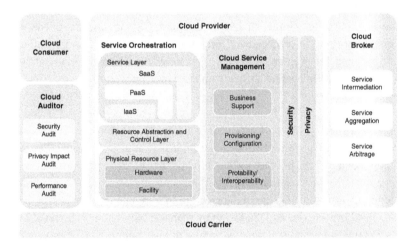

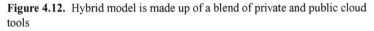

Figure 4.12. Hybrid model is made up of a blend of private and public cloud tools

Cloud computing providers serve various kinds of consumers. A cloud client might be a small business, medium business, large business, or only an individual profiting from the cloud solutions for private purposes. Irrespective of clients' types and intentions, the consumers must define their support or support requirements to the cloud suppliers, for example, storage requirements, CPU time, memory demands, accessible platforms, and software.

4.2. CLOUD-STORAGE PREREQUISITES

There's an extensive selection of accessible storage area that cloud suppliers provide, based on the client's requirements. A client may ask for only a couple of gigabytes of storage or tens of thousands of terabytes and pay a monthly or yearly charge. Cloud-storage suppliers may provide extra services and features that impact the clients' selection of a supplier. Where some suppliers, for example, offer flexible storage programs and do not have any limitations on the storage capability, other variables may impact the clients' choices. By way of example, how adaptable is information access, where a few cloud-storage suppliers firms provide smartphones accessibility to the cloud solutions; this might be an essential element for a business that needs workers obtaining services from various technologies.

4.3. CLOUD OS PREREQUISITES

A cloud OS is an OS that's intended to function in cloud computing environments. Some clients need cloud OSs to operate inside a computing-specific environment; others might use cloud OSs that offer pre-installed services and software. Typically, cloud OSs have to safely and economically operate software and hardware tools to ensure optimal delivery of solutions. Cloud browser-based OSs are all OSs that are only obtained through web browsers. This also offers the capacity for conducting a specific OS on various kinds of devices so long as the system contains an Internet browser, like smartphones. Cloud computing OSs are thought of as a SaaS because a cloud browser-based OS is your installation for applications to function as an OS for a cloud customer. Cloud OSs and cloud browser-based OSs tend to be confused with one another. Some clients need browser-based OSs to supply manageable systems which could give permissions and solutions per group or users; additional clients may call for browser-based OSs to supply utilities and applications, or VoIP solutions to network users.

4.4. MEMORY PREREQUISITES

Successful memory management is thought to be among the essential issues in cloud computing systems, in which on-demand source allocation must ensure economy in using cloud solutions. Memory has to be accessible when required rather than wasted by being allocated but not used. Amazon's EC2 is known as one of the more efficient implementations of this cloud, in which the EC2 cloud allocates the tools on demand. Many memory control methods exist which may control resource sharing among multiple virtual machines, for example, the virtual swap management mechanism (VSMM).

4.5. CPU PREREQUISITES

When clients plan to embrace cloud technology, the required CPU energy has to be given by the consumers. Comparing modern day programs CPU power could be hard. Hence, some cloud suppliers provide standardized CPU units, where every CPU unit is equivalent to some processing power of 1 GHz CPU. By way of example, a system with four CPUs that is four cores, operating at 2 GHz, will possess 32 CPU units. The standardized CPU units will help clients to plan for resource allocations and ability correctly. Cloud suppliers typically charge customers according to CPU usage or time.

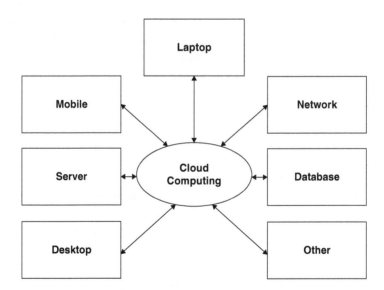

Figure 4.13. Cloud browser-based functioning system

4.6. SOFTWARE PREREQUISITES

Ensuring best utilization of tools and also their interaction with customers and solutions is attained by cloud management program. Cloud direction applications are software designed to track and function services, applications, and information in the cloud atmosphere.

The choice to embrace cloud computing solutions has to be thought out carefully by the cloud customers. Cloud computing provides several attractive alternatives, but these choices may not necessarily be beneficial or appropriate for clients regardless of the prevalence of cloud alternatives among several businesses today. Cloud solutions can be a constructive and beneficial remedy to some companies, but it may not be to other people; therefore, understanding cloud computing benefits and disadvantages is crucial before making a choice.

Cloud alternatives if appropriately implemented can generally reduce operating expenses and be quite economical. Cloud computing can lower hardware and support demands of cloud clients. Cloud computing offers freedom as resources and services could be accessed by customers everywhere. Cloud computing supports cooperation between associations. Cloud computing can provide excellent options for disaster recovery and backup programs. Cloud computing supplies highly scalable and dynamic sources. Cloud computing has lots of security vulnerabilities. Organizations adopting cloud services need to have a trusted online connection for the correct delivery of cloud solutions, and often, organizations cannot manage long downtimes. Some cloud suppliers will stop to exist. Privacy, data location, and compliance problems might happen with a few cloud suppliers. Compatibility issues might happen between the technology of the organizations as well as the cloud suppliers.

There are many security risks introduced by cloud computing. These risks are identified with the Cloud Security Alliance (CSA), which is a nonprofit organization created to specify parameters for safety advice in cloud computing (Samson 2015):

Data breaches: Attackers can make the most of a client's poorly designed database and may get to each customer's data.

Information reduction: Many problems may cause information loss, for example, attackers, careless providers, or crises.

Account or support traffic hijacking: Several malicious activities by attackers can be achieved in this area; a few cases are given below:

a. Gain access to customers' credentials
b. Manipulate information
c. Redirect customers to unethical sites
d. Create in the client's system a new foundation for launching other strikes

Insecure interfaces and APIs: IT admins rely on ports for cloud monitoring and management. APIs are essential to safety and access to general cloud providers. Thus, third parties and parties on several events are proven to build these ports and inject advertising solutions or additional applications.

Denial of service (DoS) attacks: DoS attacks may lead to accessibility issues to one or more solutions. DoS attacks can cost clients significant losses.

Malicious insiders: this could be workers employed within the cloud providers or contractors with malicious intentions who might cause harm to both the clients and the cloud supplier.

Some examples of cloud misuse:

a. A customer utilizing the cloud support to break an encryption key that is too hard to crack using a local computer.
b. A customer intending to establish a DoS attack, disperses malware or some other prohibited action over a non-local cloud-based network.

Before the adoption of cloud solutions, organizations need to understand and establish the cloud computing safety dangers, and make a logical choice on whether the business should use cloud computing technology or not. This should include how cloud computing can provide the best benefits, and what safety measures have to be obtained.

Common technology vulnerabilities are present at each stage of delivering model to get a cloud service supplier where a compromised part (like applications, a stage, or infrastructure) may impact the entire network. Other kinds of security risks associated with ownership of information, shared access, isolation collapse, and virtual distributions also exist.

Although significant and various security dangers exist, this should not stop businesses from embracing the attractive advantages of cloud computing. The safety risks should be taken under consideration and precautions have to be taken. Cloud computing is now a multibillion-dollar business, and many businesses, organizations, and cooperatives have adopted cloud computing solutions and advantages (Durbano et al. 2010; Trivedi and Pasley 2012; Beal 2018; Agape Consulting Group 2016). Clients should realize that a secure network does not exist, but the safety breaches of cloud computing may be mitigated to attain a fantastic degree of safety. A client may apply the next measures:

1. Identifying the dangers of moving into the cloud
2. Instituting fantastic compliance, security, and privacy policies, and ensuring the appliance of the coverages with concerned parties
3. Assessing the safety responsibilities of the client and cloud supplier
4. Making sure auditing of operational solutions is carried out

5. Assessing the security steps of the cloud supplier
6. Making sure the correct protection of information and solutions is applied
7. Knowing safety measures related to the company relationship together with the cloud supplier is applied

Cloud computing is a desirable alternative for businesses, providing many advantages and alternatives, and continues to be widely adopted by companies. It gives efficacy and cost-saving advantages, thus enabling companies to concentrate on their core purposes. The companies must undertake minimal capital investments in their data centers and data technologies. Cloud computing has become a multibillion-dollar business and is expected to continue growing; however, there are worries, and also the most crucial concern is safety. Cloud computing sellers have started to tackle the security issues of their customers, but we know that safety is still a dynamic and evolving attribute using almost any service provider.

REFERENCES

Agape Consulting Group. 2016. "Cloud Computing Glossary of Terms." https://agapeconsultinggroup.com/2016/10/10/cloud-computing-glossary-of-terms/

Beal, V. 2018. "What is Thin Client?," *Webopedia*. https://www.webopedia.com/TERM/T/thin_client.html

Durbano, J.P., D. Rustvold, G. Saylor, and J. Studarus. 2010. "Securing the Cloud." In *Cloud Computing: Principles, Systems and Applications*, eds. N. Antonoupolos and L. Gillam. London, England: Springer, pp. 289–302.

Hayes, B. 2008. "Cloud Computing." *Communications of ACM* 51, no. 7, pp. 9–11.

Hofer, M., and G. Howanitz. 2009. "The Client Side of Cloud Computing, University of Salzbrg, Austria.". https://www.routledgehandbooks.com/pdf/doi/10.1201/9781315372112-19

Samson, T. 2015. "9 Top Threats to Cloud Computing Security," *InfoWorld*. https://downloads.cloudsecurityalliance.org/assets/research/top-threats/top-threats-to-cloud-computing-deep-dive.pdf

Trivedi, K., and K. Pasley. 2012. *Cloud Computing Security*. Indianapolis, IN: Cisco Press.

CHAPTER 5

Cloud Computing Security Essentials

The evolution of the Internet can be divided into three productions: from the 1970s, the first production has been marked by expensive mainframe computers obtained from terminals; the second generation was born in the late 1980s and early 1990s and has been identified from the explosion of personal computers with graphical user interfaces (GUIs). The first decade of the nineteenth century introduced the third creation, defined by mobile computing—the Internet of Things—and cloud computing.

In 1997, Prof. Ramnath Chellappa of Emory University defined cloud computing systems for the first time, calling it an important "computing paradigm in which the boundaries of computing is going to be set by economic rationale instead of technical limitations alone."

Even though the international IT literature and media have come forward since then with many definitions, models, and architectures for cloud computing, autonomic and utility computing systems were the basis of the community commonly referred to as cloud computing. From the early 2000s, firms began quickly embracing this concept upon the realization that cloud computing may benefit both the providers and the consumers of services. Businesses started delivering computing functionality via the Internet, enterprise-level applications, web-based retail services, document-sharing capacities, and entirely hosted IT platforms, to mention just a few of the cloud computing applications of the 2000s. The hottest widespread adoption of virtualization and service-oriented architecture (SOA) has promulgated cloud computing as a fundamental and increasingly significant part of any delivery and critical-mission strategy. It enables existing and new products and services to be provided and absorbed much more effectively, conveniently, and safely. Unsurprisingly, cloud computing became one of the hottest trends in IT, with unique and complementary properties, such as elasticity, resiliency, quick provisioning, and multitenancy. Information systems are currently at a triple or three-factor inflexion point in IT's development (Figure 5.1).

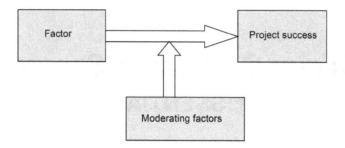

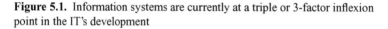

Figure 5.1. Information systems are currently at a triple or 3-factor inflexion point in the IT's development

Virtualization of computing infrastructure sets the Lee Chao model for cloud computing for instruction and learning: Strategies for both implementation and design, University of Houston-Victoria, USA, 1--357, 2012. This is the foundation for its technical inflexion point, providing ubiquitous cloud computing which nurtured the development of pervasive freedom and rapid growth of the Internet of Things (IoT) or Network of Things (NoT). Cloud computing, mobility, and IoT/NoT would be the steering elements that induced the business operations inflexion point, transforming the world from connected to hyper-connected. Owing to its resilience and expandable capacity offered at a reduced price, cloud computing resources became the target and the source of malicious actions, triggering an expansion among attackers and inducing an inflection in the elegance and strength of strikes, causing the exponential growth of cybercrimes.

5.1. CLOUD COMPUTING DEFINITION

According to the definition published in NIST Special Publication (SP) 800-115:

> Cloud computing is a model for empowering ubiquitous, convenient, on-demand network access into a shared pool of configurable computing resources (e.g., networks, servers, storage, software, and services) that may be quickly provisioned and introduced with minimal management effort or service provider interaction.

Enterprises may use these resources to develop, host, and operate applications and services on demand in a manner that is flexible anytime, anyplace, and on any device. This definition is widely recognized as providing a clear understanding of cloud computing technologies and cloud solutions and has been submitted as the U.S. contribution for global standardization.

The U.S. National Institute of Standards and Technology (NIST) provided the widely adopted definition of cloud computing which also identifies its most essential features—deployment and support models. According to the description published in NIST Special Publication (SP) 800-115:

> Cloud computing is a model for enabling ubiquitous, convenient, on-demand community access to a shared pool of configurable computing resources (e.g., networks, servers and storage, applications, and services) that may be quickly provisioned and introduced with minimal management effort or service supplier interaction.

Enterprises can use these resources to develop, host, and run applications and services on demand in a flexible manner anytime, anywhere, and on any device. This definition is widely recognized as providing an evident understanding of cloud computing technology and cloud solutions and has been submitted as the U.S. participation in international standardization.

The NIST definition also provides a unifying view of five fundamental qualities of cloud services: on-demand self-explanatory, broad network accessibility, resource allocation, rapid elasticity, and quantified support. When coupled, a service model and installation model categorize ways to provide cloud services. NIST SP 800-115 defines the three service models as follows:

1. **IaaS:** The capability provided to the consumer would be to supply processing, networks, storage, and other fundamental computing resources where the user can deploy and run the random software, which may include things like operating systems and software. The consumer does not manage or control the underlying cloud infrastructure, but has control over operating systems, storage, deployed applications, and possibly limited control of picking networking components (e.g., server firewalls).

2. **PaaS:** The capability provided to the consumer would be to set up consumer-created or acquired software on the cloud infrastructure which is created using programming tools and languages supported by the provider. The consumer does not manage or control the

underlying cloud infrastructure, such as network, servers, operating systems, or storage, but has control over the installed software and possibly the application-hosting environment configurations.

3. **SaaS:** The capacity given to the consumer is to use the provider's software working on a cloud infrastructure. The applications are accessible from several client devices via a thin client interface, such as a web browser (e.g., online e-mail). The user does not control or manage the internal cloud infrastructure, including network, servers, operating systems, storage, as well as individual program capabilities, with the possible exception of limited user-specific application configuration settings.

ISO/IEC JTC1 SC38 WG3 and ITU-T also developed a cloud computing taxonomy that is derived from NIST SP 800-115: International Standard ISO/IEC 17788, recommendation ITU-T Y.3500 Information technologies—Cloud computing—Summary and vocabulary. The first notions of cloud computing and many of the terms are mostly interchangeable between the NIST and ISO/IEC standards. But since NIST's cloud computing definition has been available for a longer period and constitutes the core concept characterized by an ISO/IEC standard, this book references the NIST definition. All the three cloud support models have the following capabilities:

- IaaS enables cloud consumers to conduct almost any operating systems and software of their choice on the hardware and resource abstraction layers (hypervisors) supplied by the cloud supplier. A consumer's operating systems and software can be migrated into the cloud supplier's hardware, possibly replacing an organization's data center infrastructure.
- PaaS allows consumers to produce their cloud applications. The cloud supplier leaves a virtualized environment and a set of resources to allow the creation of new web applications.
- SaaS enables cloud consumers to conduct online applications. Off-the-shelf programs are accessed over the Internet. The cloud provider owns the software, and the consumers are authorized to use the following services after an agreement signed between parties.

In summary, cloud computing gives a handy, on-demand way to access a shared pool of configurable resources (e.g., networks, servers, storage, programs, and solutions), enabling users to develop, host, and operate applications and services on demand in a flexible manner anytime, anywhere, and on any device.

NIST was also the first to specify a technology and implementation agnostic cloud computing reference architecture (RA) (NIST SP 500-292) that identifies the most critical cloud actors, their functions, as well as the main architectural elements required for managing and supplying cloud solutions (e.g., service deployment, service orchestration, service management, service aggregation).

Derived from NIST SP 500-292, ISO/IEC JTC1 SC38 WG3, also ITU-T also developed a benchmark architecture standard: International Standard ISO/IEC 17789 | Recommendation ITU-T Y.3502 Information technology—Cloud computing—reference structure* that describes cloud computing actors, focusing on cloud provider and cloud customer, while grouping the other cloud actors in another cloud partner's class. Cloud RAs plus a cloud taxonomy are foundational documents which assist cloud computing stakeholders to communicate concepts, structure, or operational and security requirements, to enumerate only a few of their benefits. As emphasized previously, the cloud RA is a generic, high-level conceptual design that facilitates the understanding of cloud computing's operational intricacies. The RA does not signify the system structure of a specific cloud computing system; instead, it is a tool for describing, discussing, and creating a system-specific architecture using a common framework of reference.

The architecture depicted in Figure 5.2 is not tied to any specific vendor products, solutions, or benchmark implementations, nor does it

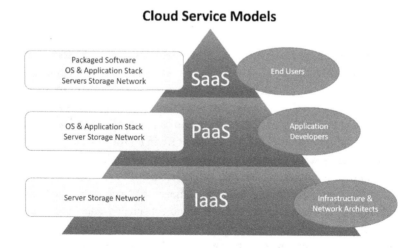

Figure 5.2. Cloud architecture, NIST cloud computing security RA strategy
Source: NIST 2011b.

provide prescriptive solutions. The RA defines a group of cloud actors, and their activities, and functions that could be utilized for orchestrating a cloud ecosystem. The cloud computing RA relates to some companion cloud computing taxonomy and has a set of descriptions and views which are the foundation for talking about the features, applications, and standards.

Moreover, the NIST RA diagram explains, for each cloud actor, the overall activities in a cloud ecosystem. This RA is meant to ease the understanding of the operational intricacies of computing. It does not represent the system structure of a specific cloud computing system; instead, it is a tool for describing, discussing, and developing a particular system architecture employing a standard frame of reference, which we intend to leverage in our later discussion of critical management issues in a cloud environment. To enhance the NIST SP 500-292 cloud RA, NIST identified in NIST SP 500-299, cloud security reference structure, two types of cloud brokers:

- Business broker, and
- Technical broker.

To enhance the NIST SP 500-292 cloud RA, in NIST SP 500-299, cloud security reference architecture (see Figure 5.2), NIST identified two types of cloud providers, as well as the crucial management functions which fall under the provider's responsibilities. These may need to be divided between the two suppliers, based on the architectural aspects of the cloud service. From the cloud customer's standpoint, this segregation is not visible. The leading provider offers services hosted on an infrastructure it owns. It might make these services available to customers via a third party (like a broker or intermediary provider), but the defining characteristic of a primary provider is the fact that it does not acquire the sources of its support offerings from other providers. An intermediary supplier can interact with other cloud providers without offering visibility or transparency to the principal provider(s). An intermediary provider uses services provided by the leading provider as invisible elements of its service, which it presents to the customer as an integrated offering. From a security standpoint, all safety services and components required of a critical provider are also required of an intermediary provider (NIST 2011b, 2013).

A company broker only provides company and connection services and does not have any contact with the cloud consumer's data, operations, or artifacts (e.g., pictures, volumes, firewalls) from the cloud and, thus, has no responsibilities in executing any crucial management functions, regardless of the cloud structure. Conversely, a technical agent does interact with a customer's assets; the specialized broker aggregates services from multiple cloud suppliers and provides a layer of technical functionality by fixing a single point of entry and interoperability problems. There are two critical defining characteristics of a professional cloud agent which are distinct from an intermediary provider:

1. The capability to provide a single consistent interface (for business or technical functions) to numerous differing providers, and
2. The clear visibility the agent allows into who is supplying the services in the background as opposed to intermediary providers who do not offer you such transparency.

Since the technical broker permits this clear visibility, the customer knows which cloud capacities are employed by the professional agent versus those provided by the cloud provider(s) working together with the technical broker.

This case is different from the one in which an intermediary supplier is involved, since the intermediary supplier is opaque, and the consumer is unaware of how the essential management functions are split, when applicable, between the intermediary supplier and the principal supplier.

5.2. CLOUD COMPUTING SECURITY ESSENTIALS

Cloud computing provides partnerships with substantial cost savings, both concerning capital expenditures (CAPEX) and operating expenses (OPEX), and also allows them to leverage leading-edge technology to meet their data processing needs. In a cloud environment, security and privacy are a cross-cutting concern for all cloud actors, because both touch upon most of the layers of the cloud computing RA and affect many pieces of cloud support. Hence, the safety management of these resources associated with cloud services is a vital aspect of computing. In a cloud surrounding, you will find security threats, and security requirements that differ for distinct cloud installation models, along with the significant mitigations against such threats and cloud celebrity responsibilities for implementing security controls rely upon the support model selected, and the service categories that were chosen.

A number of the security risks could be mitigated with the application of standard security procedures and mechanisms, while some require cloud-specific solutions. Since every layer of the cloud computing RA may have different security vulnerabilities and might be subjected to unique threats, the structure of a cloud-enabled service directly affects its security position and the machine's key management aspects.

Figure 5.3 uses a building block approach to depict a graphical representation of the cloud consumer's visibility and availability of the numerous layers of a cloud atmosphere. As the figure shows, within an IaaS service version, the cloud user has high profile into everything over the application program interface (API) layer, while the cloud suppliers implement controls below the API layer (that are usually opaque to customers).

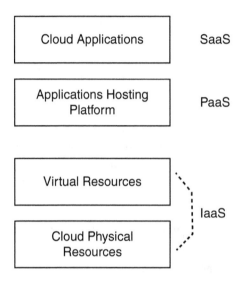

Figure 5.3. Uses a building block approach to depict a graphical representation of the cloud consumer's visibility and availability of the numerous layers of a cloud atmosphere

The cloud user has restricted visibility and central restricted management control in a PaaS version because the cloud provider implements the security functions in all layers below the integration and middleware layer.

The cloud consumer loses control and visibility in a SaaS model, and generally, controls below the presentation layer are opaque to the cloud user, because the cloud supplier implements all security functions. While all cloud actors involved in orchestrating a cloud ecosystem are responsible for fixing operational, security and privacy concerns, cloud consumers retain the information ownership and so remain fully accountable for

- Properly identifying data's sensitivity
- Assessing the threat from any vulnerability or abuse of the data and the impact to their business

- Defining security requirements commensurable with the data sensitivity
- Approving necessary risk mitigations

Some of those cloud consumers areas of concern are

- Risk management
- Business continuity
- Disaster recovery plans
- Restoration plan integrating and quantifying the recovery point objective and recovery time objective for services

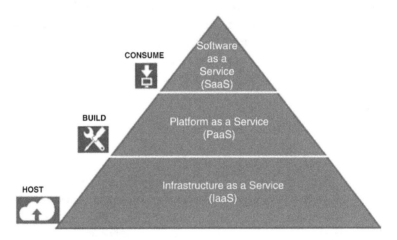

Figure 5.4. Consumer's level of control

- Physical and environmental security policy
- Physical security
- Contingency strategy
- Emergency response plan
- Core design
- Safety infrastructure
- Human resources
- Environmental safety
- Visual inspection of the facility

User account termination procedures should be compliant with national and international industry standards on safety. There must be a transparent view of the security position of the cloud providers, agents, and carriers.

Technological advancements have contributed to cloud computing's development as a viable choice for meeting the technology needs of numerous organizations. However, for cloud consumers to grasp the whole benefit of cloud computing economies of scale, flexibility, and its full potential, consumers will need to address the issues listed above and quantify the risk associated with the adoption of a cloud-based data system.

Cloud computing protection denotes the set of processes, processes, and criteria designed to give information security assurance in a cloud ecosystem. On the flip side, these same technical resources, as well as the massive concentration of data, present an attractive target to attackers. Cloud computing security addresses both physical and logical security issues across all the various service models of software, platform, and infrastructure. It also addresses how these services are delivered to the general public, private, hybrid vehicle, and community delivery models. The new economic model facilitated by cloud computing technology has driven substantial technological changes for cloud-based information systems concerning scale, architecture, safety, and privacy:

- **Scale:** The commoditization of cloud computing along with the organizations' push toward economic efficiency have led to enormous concentrations of hardware tools necessary to provide those services.

- **Architecture:** On-demand utilization of computing resources, the tools abstraction from the underlying components, and also the multitenancy that brings together unrelated people or organizations who share hardware and software tools are only a few specific characteristics of this relatively new technology. Massively distributed computing, content storage, and data processing relying solely on rational isolation mechanisms to safeguard it are also characteristics of cloud computing. Global markets for commodities require advantage distribution networks where content is sent and received as close to the customers as possible. This tendency toward international distribution and redundancy provides increased resilience for its cloud-based data systems while, on the downside, it means the resources are usually managed in physical and logical bulk .

- **Safety:** The centralization of data and increase in security-focused resources may improve safety, but concerns can persist for losing control of specific sensitive information, and the absence of security for stored kernels. Safety is often as good as or better than traditional systems, in part because suppliers can devote resources to solving safety problems that many customers cannot afford to tackle. On the other hand, the complexity of safety considerably increases when data has to be distributed over a broader area or over more than a significant quantity of devices, as well as in multitenant systems shared by unrelated users. Additionally, user access to safety audit logs might be difficult or impossible for cloud suppliers to give to cloud consumers. Personal cloud installations are in part inspired by users' desire to retain control over the infrastructure and also to prevent losing control of information security.

• **Privacy:** Cloud computing owns privacy issues since the providers have access to this information that is saved in their infrastructure. Cloud providers could accidentally or intentionally alter or even delete info. Many cloud providers can share information with third parties if needed without a warrant. The consent is granted in their privacy policy, which users consent to before they start utilizing cloud services. Privacy options include policy and legislation as well as end users' choices for how data are saved. Users can encrypt data which are processed or stored in the cloud to stop unauthorized access.

Because different users are utilizing a cloud provider platform, there may be a possibility of information belonging to various clients residing on the same information server. Consequently, information leakage may arise unintentionally when data for one client is given to another client. Additionally, hackers spend substantial time and effort searching for methods to locate vulnerabilities in the cloud infrastructure that would allow them to penetrate the cloud. Because data from hundreds or thousands of organizations can be kept on big cloud servers, hackers may theoretically gain control of enormous stores of data through a single attack of the hypervisor—a process known as hyperjacking.

Another cloud ecosystem issue is the legal possession of this data and the obligations and rights of the information owner and information custodian. Since cloud users maintain ownership of the information residing in a cloud ecosystem, they usually maintain the safety authorization in-house and are also responsible for identifying all safety requirements about the cloud ecosystem's hosting and processing of those data.

But because a cloud consumer's level of management and control of this cloud ecosystem's heap is restricted by the adopted cloud architecture (see discussion associated with Figure 5.3), cloud providers and cloud technical brokers (when involved) become the information custodians and are responsible for fulfilling all safety and privacy requirements identified by the cloud user. It is always recommended that the cloud consumers review the implementation of the privacy and security controls and make sure that all the requirements are met before authorizing the use of a cloud-based information system.

5.3. DIVIDING OPERATIONAL RESPONSIBILITIES

Once a cloud consumer selects the most suitable cloud structure and defines another cloud celebrity partner to orchestrate the ecosystem, all actors must work together to identify their operational duties. These responsibilities are often split among actors with the level of responsibility shifting based on the deployment and service models adopted. The cloud consumer should be ultimately responsible for specifying the security and privacy controls required to safeguard the data and cloud-based information system. The implementation of many of these controls is frequently the duty of the cloud suppliers or technical cloud brokers (when involved). When the cloud architecture is defined, cloud actors engaged in orchestrating the ecosystem identify the management ports exposed to cloud customers. Examples of control interfaces that a cloud supplier and broker can disclose are:

- System, security, and program logs
- Broker APIs for instrumentation
- The broker's web application for handling cloud customer applications

Ultimately, each cloud celebrity is responsible for his or her various operational activities as defined in the safety authority for the cloud-based information platform.

Below the cloud computing paradigm, a company relinquishes direct control over many elements of security and privacy, and in doing so, confers a high degree of confidence on the cloud supplier(s) along with the cloud technical broker. At the same time, cloud consumers, as data owners, have a duty to protect data and data systems commensurate with the risk and magnitude of the harm resulting from unauthorized access, use, disclosure, disruption, modification, or destruction, irrespective of whether the information is collected or maintained by or on behalf of their cloud user.

To be able to keep confidence in the cloud ecosystem and adequately mitigate risks associated with the cloud-based information systems, cloud actors need visibility into one another's area.

Transition to cloud computing solutions involves a transfer of responsibility to execute necessary privacy and security controls to the cloud providers and technical cloud brokers for securing portions of the system on which the cloud customer's data and applications operate. Visibility into how the cloud supplier functions, such as the provisioning of composite solutions, is an essential ingredient for adequate oversight of system safety and privacy by a cloud consumer.

To make sure that policy and procedures have been enforced through-out the system life cycle, service arrangements must include some means for your organization to be able to see the security and privacy controls and procedures utilized by the cloud provider and their performance over time.

Trust is an important concept related to risk management. The reliance on cloud computing solutions results in the demand for trust relationships among cloud actors. But, building trustworthiness requires visibility into suppliers' and technical brokers' practices and risk/information security decisions to properly gauge the threat and estimate the risk tolerance. It is critical to say that the level of trust can vary and the accepted risk depends on the established trust relationship. The next section further discusses the importance of creating trust and introduces the idea of confidence border. Additionally, Chapter 7 discusses in detail the cloud consumer's risk man-agement in a cloud ecosystem.

In a cloud ecosystem, it is of crucial importance for cloud users to establish the apparent demarcation of information system boundaries on all levels within a vendor-neutral method. Furthermore, it is incumbent on the cloud user to develop measures to ensure proper protection, irrespec-tive of vendor, ownership, or support level for the cloud-based information system. To avoid vendor lock-in and to allow for a vigilant improvement of designed countermeasures, cloud consumers must not only set a plan to adopt a cloud-based solution but also be ready to transition to alternate cloud suppliers or brokers if necessary.

Accordingly, at every level along with the subsystem level, a cloud user should identify the safety and privacy controls and negotiate which cloud celebrity is responsible for the implementation and operation of each control function. Every cloud actor should track and manage the service levels and the licensure, and should also want to support the integrity and availability of the data system on a boundary-by-boundary basis. Furthermore, if topical integrations to the cloud service provide performance, data feeds, or services, all strata needs to be identified and the information system control border must be established. Also, for the aggregated cloud service, cloud actors need to develop clear possession of the methodology to preserve, track, and protect the provided performance, the transactions, along with the associated data.

The practice of establishing information system boundaries and the related risk management implications remains an organization-wide ac-tivity independent of seller interaction. Cloud customers will need to carefully negotiate with all actors participating in the orchestration of the cloud ecosystem solutions for all of a company's business requirements, all intricate technical concerns with respect to data security, and the pro-grammatic costs to the business. To construct the foundational degree of protection for the information and to provide the adequate overall security position of this cloud-based data system, the inherited security and privacy controls implemented by cloud providers and cloud technical agents (when participating in the orchestration) need to be correctly assessed and monitored at each boundary. To elevate the programs' security position and protect data commensurable with its sensitivity, cloud users often should negotiate tailoring of current controls via parameter choice or via implementation of compensating safety and privacy controls.

Because data owners retain the responsibility and accountability to ensure that all of cloud security controls are handled and monitored on a continuing basis, it is essential to incorporate in the safety programs and the service agreements, clear grasp of, and attention to

- The choice, implementation, evaluation, and tracking of safety controls for cloud-based systems
- The consequences of modifications in the cloud support performance on the overall security position of the cloud-based data system and about the assignment and business processes supported by that system
- The effects of changes to the information system onto the cloud service and its controls.

Security controls identified by the cloud user and employed by cloud actors are documented in the safety plan for its holistic data system and assessed for effectiveness throughout the risk management process (i.e., during the first authorization of the data system and subsequently during the constant monitoring process).

Cloud security controls can also be assessed for efficacy if a further functionality is added after the data system is approved to operate. As owners of this data, cloud consumers need to take suitable measures to ensure that changes in any internal boundary of the cloud system do not affect the safety posture of the general system.

Furthermore, they have to aggregate, in the information level, applications, platforms, and infrastructure level, all pertinent information obtained from the cloud providers and technical cloud brokers, and to consolidate the aggregated data, behavior near real-time observation and execute safety impact analyses.

The following sections identify and discuss each physical or logical border in the cloud ecosystem. When architecting a cloud-based information system and orchestrating the cloud ecosystem, the cloud consumer should start by categorizing the consumer's data along with the application and differentiating the corresponding boundaries. Then, the consumer should identify functional capacities or components that are needed to support the implementation and secure the information, the multiple bounds corresponding to the service model, the cloud ecosystem's orchestration, the cloud installation model, and last, but not the least, the trust boundary. In the next sections, we discuss these bounds.

5.4. USER-DATA BOUNDARY

The core of the cloud ecosystem would be the user-data boundary. This border traverses all stackable practical layers of the cloud ecosystem, which also comprises the cloud customers' information, which defines the necessary level of security in all outer layers.

The way the user-data boundary intersects with the demonstration, API, and application border helps us understand the value of the information stored inside the user-data midsize and the corresponding safety controls required to operate the said outer operational layers. The middle of this cloud ecosystem, the user-data boundary (Figure 5.5) includes user information encompassed within the user-data perimeter. As the user information contained inside the user-data perimeter goes from cloud supplier to cloud customer, the user-data boundary traverses the demonstration, the API, along with the application boundary and should guarantee the safety of the information.

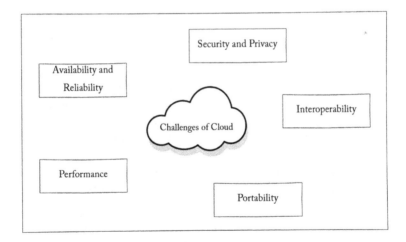

Figure 5.5. User-data boundary

A data-centric architecture leveraging a border strategy warrants that all elements of a cloud ecosystem are designed and instrumented based on the sensitivity of the cloud customers' data.

Service border is a general concept introduced to identify the support layers obtained by employing a cloud consumer or employed by cloud actors other than the consumer.

Data-centric boundaries

- SaaS border
- Demo modality boundary
- Display platform border
- Application programming interfaces boundary
- Applications boundary
- Data boundary
- Metadata boundary
- Content border
- IaaS boundary
- Software programming interfaces border
- Core connectivity and delivery boundary
- Abstraction boundary
- Hardware boundary
- Facilities border

These sections discuss critical components of border definition and acceptable risk. Since the consumer's view is offered in these sections, the performance the consumer manages is perceived as inner, and also to better emphasize the data-centric structure with layers wrapping around user's data, the bounds defining customer's managed layers are referred to as internal service bounds.

In contrast, the boundaries defining the layers led by other cloud actors (supplier, technical agent, etc.) are declared as outer service bounds. Additionally, because of the similarities in graphical representation between the three kinds of service bounds, only a graphical representation of your PaaS boundaries is supplied below.

The capability provided to the [cloud consumer] is to supply processing, storage, networks, and other fundamental computing tools where the consumer can deploy and run arbitrary software, which can include things like operating systems and software. The [cloud consumer] does not manage or control the underlying cloud infrastructure but has control over operating systems, storage, and deployed applications; and may be limited control of select networking elements (e.g., host firewalls).

You will find both internal and external boundaries, which the cloud consumer needs to establish with the cloud provider to delineate management control and range of responsibilities.

The IaaS boundary divides the cloud ecosystem in the infrastructure layer exposing as an agency the IaaS API, while outlining the layers barred to customers since the interconnected stack encompasses core connectivity, hardware, and facilities. Beyond the IaaS border lies the ecosystem orchestration boundary, cloud installation boundary, and trust boundary. The internal and external IaaS boundaries require coordination to establish a decent level of trust and to coordinate security with other cloud actors. This trust has to be determined with all the IaaS whether the agency is provided within the customer's control or not. Well-defined boundaries must delineate responsibilities for security, privacy, and high quality of providers within the service boundaries.

Consumers need to assess the trustworthiness of interfaces (logical and physical) with other actors both inside and outside system boundaries. The cloud deployment version chosen from the cloud user has a direct impact on the trust relationship with the cloud provider(s). For the IaaS support model, the cloud user assumes a higher level of responsibility than the cloud provider or other actors for the support provided.

PaaS Security Boundaries NIST SP 800-115 defined PaaS as follows:

- The capacity given to the [cloud consumer] would be to deploy onto the [cloud supplier] consumer-created or obtained applications generated by using programming language, libraries, services, and tools supported by the provider. The [cloud consumer] does not manage or control the underlying cloud infrastructure including network, servers, operating systems, or storage, but he commands within the deployed applications and possibly configuration settings for the application-hosting environment.
- The PaaS border divides the cloud ecosystem in the platform layer offering an integrated development environment and integration stage, while delineating the layers external to consumers as the connected stack that packs servers, network, operation systems, and storage, from the operating environment down to facilities, allowing cloud customers to deploy or construct their selection of compatible applications. Like the IaaS service bounds, a PaaS-based ecosystem includes PaaS internal and external boundaries, which the cloud user establishes with the cloud supplier to delineate management control and range of duties. Providers assume increasing amounts of responsibility for implementing and monitoring security.

Figure 5.6 depicts the PaaS outer boundaries consisting of an interconnected stack that connects the facility boundaries of this IaaS with the integration boundary of the PaaS. Below the PaaS, limits establish the API, the delivery and connectivity, both the abstraction and control, as well as the hardware and amenities bounds. The limitations that supply PaaS interfaces require coordination to establish an acceptable level of trust and coordination of security together with the cloud provider. As mentioned previously, cloud users will

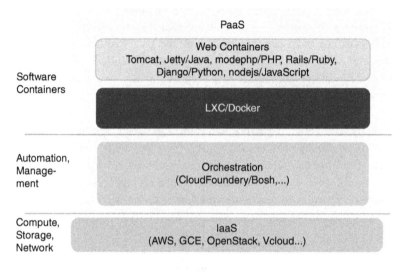

Figure 5.6. Platform-as-a-service border—supplier's layers

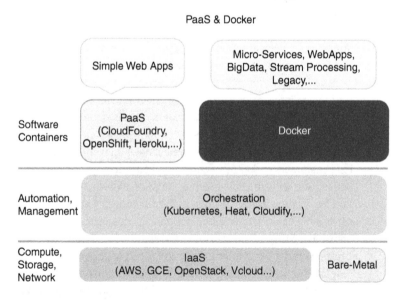

Figure 5.7. Deployment border with PaaS external layers. Platform-as-a-service boundary—consumer's layers

need to estimate the danger of using the system and establish the risk tolerance. Cloud providers, in most cases, assume increased responsibility for safety and support coordination than cloud customers in a PaaS established cloud ecosystem.

SaaS Security Boundaries NIST SP 800-115 defines SaaS as follows:

- The capability provided to this [cloud consumer] is to use the [cloud provider's] applications running [in a cloud ecosystem managed by the supplier or technical broker]. The applications are accessible from various client devices through either a thin client interface, like a web browser (e.g., web-based e-mail) or a software interface. [Cloud users] don't manage or control the internal cloud [ecosystem] including network, servers, operating systems, storage, or perhaps individual program capacities, with the possible exception of limited user-specific application configuration settings.
- Cloud providers must assume the most significant level of responsibility for fulfilling all common compliance requirements and for monitoring and implementing security and privacy controls. The SaaS border divides the cloud ecosystem in the software layer exposing as support the program and SaaS API(s) while delineating the layers outside to consumers as the interconnected pile that encompasses from the software layer down to facilities.

The internal SaaS boundaries consist of an interconnected stack of top layer borders that include the consumer data, demonstration, API, and program. The SaaS outer boundaries begin at the SaaS coating and build upon PaaS outer boundaries. The bounds that expose ports at the SaaS layer require operational, safety, and privacy coordination with the cloud supplier to establish a decent level of trust. Trust in a SaaS-based cloud ecosystem needs to be created by the cloud consumer in concert with any contracted cloud actors (suppliers, agents, etc.). Within the SaaS boundaries, establishing trust is not only harder but is also a more critical component because the provider is assuming most and sometimes all of the responsibilities for deploying and managing the process. Since the support is outside the cloud consumer's physical or logical control, establishing and maintaining trust could only be done through well-defined deployment and orchestration bounds with enforceable terms and conditions. Relative to the IaaS and PaaS service models, within a SaaS-based cloud ecosystem, cloud providers assume the best response for implementing privacy and security controls and organizing and managing the service.

The amount of confidence within SaaS boundaries and between the internal and external SaaS boundaries—for both the cloud consumer and the cloud provider—ought to be the most viable, and therefore more restrictive service arrangements and SLAs are demanded, together with well-defined penalties and liabilities.

5.5. ECOSYSTEM ORCHESTRATION BOUNDARY

To minimize business expenses and reduce the price of cloud solutions, providers design cloud solution sets targeting as many prospective customers as possible. Such solutions are more accessible for business segments to understand and transfer workloads within, and to, the cloud. These pre-packaged solution sets frequently contain modules of elements that are identical, with identical settings, and that can easily be reproducible in different cloud ecosystems.

This chapter described the cloud ecosystem as an intricate system of interdependent components that work together to allow a cloud-based information system. It is essential to be aware that while serving a cloud-based information system, a cloud ecosystem could be orchestrated by multiple cloud actors that collaborate to build it.

Cloud providers construct the foundation of the ecosystem. The layers assembled by agents or intermediate providers inherit the controls from the lower sheets from the stack implemented by providers. Based on the support model, a cloud user adds performance to the cloud ecosystem, while inheriting privacy and security controls achieved by all other cloud actors.

Many times, due to the multitenancy character of cloud computing systems, components of the cloud ecosystem have been shared with all other cloud ecosystems serving different information systems. Moreover, except for an on-premises personal cloud, many clouds operate in third-party data centers. And in an on-premises personal cloud, there are likely to be provisions for cloudburst to a different cloud under extreme conditions. Among the impediments to broader cloud computing adoption is the cloud consumers' inability to continuously monitor the controls employed by new cloud actors or the operation of the elements managed by these actors.

By ensuring that all of the cloud actors have a clear comprehension of their responsibilities and that the cloud actors correctly implement agreed-upon security and privacy controls identified in the safety plans, it is feasible for the cloud actors to define the cloud ecosystem orchestration boundary and to accurately assess the inherited risk from the usage of the particular orchestration for the information system under discussion.

Orchestration of this cloud ecosystem allows private, public, and hybrid vehicles to operate with elasticity, scale, and efficiency.

The ecosystem orchestration boundary is recognized if the decisions are made to include certain cloud actors and also to establish their responsibilities. For instance, a cloud ecosystem might be supported by a single cloud provider that offers its services to a cloud consumer. Alternatively, a similar SaaS-based ecosystem might be architected such that services from several cloud providers are aggregated by a technical broker and offered to some cloud consumer within a SaaS-based information platform. In specific instances, cloud users may prefer to acquire more control within the cloud ecosystem and so choose to leverage PaaS or even IaaS solutions to construct a similar data system by adding the necessary functional layers into the PaaS or even IaaS offer, writing a final SaaS-like solution.

The ecosystem orchestration boundary should incorporate automated workflow operation and management of their cloud ecosystem's elements

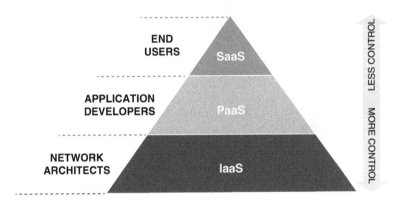

Figure 5.8. Ecosystem orchestration boundary, IaaS, PaaS, SaaS, and user-data borders

(e.g., computer, individuality, credentials, and access management). A cloud celebrity that orchestrates the cloud ecosystem needs to ensure that all cloud resources serving an information system along with their configuration management capabilities are identified and placed inside the ecosystem orchestration boundary for the proper assessment of the inherited risk and adequate continuous monitoring. Cloud orchestration is complicated because it involves bookkeeping for automation of interrelated procedures running across heterogeneous systems, possibly in some places. Often processes and transactions might need to cross numerous businesses, networks, methods, and boundary-protection devices. The orchestration purpose is a high-priority goal from a hazard standpoint. Accurately identifying all orchestration parts and including them within the cloud ecosystem orchestration border to be accounted for and detailed in the information system security program is crucial.

5.6. DEPLOYMENT BOUNDARY

Once the cloud ecosystem orchestration border is established, the next logical step is to select the cloud installation model which best meets the cloud consumer's needs. The four kinds of cloud deployment versions are personal, public, hybrid, and community.

A cloud installation border is a logical boundary, which gives a common framework for analyzing the level of exclusivity the cloud consumer needs in your cloud-based information system. Often the data program's impact level pushes the last decision regarding the cloud installation model. In Figure 5.9, the cloud installation boundary is represented as constituting each of the components contained therein, for example, ecosystem orchestration boundary, IaaS, PaaS, SaaS, and user-data borders.

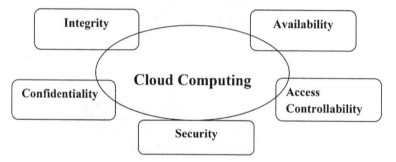

Figure 5.9. Depicts the trust boundary as the surface of the bounds. Trust border—notion explained

- **Private:** The cloud infrastructure is operated for the exclusive use of a single owner. The owning organization could handle the cloud instance or work with a third party.
- **Public:** The cloud's infrastructure is readily available for public use, alternatively for a large business group and is possessed by an organization selling cloud solutions.
- **Community:** A cloud instance was supplied that has been organized to serve a common purpose or function.
- **Hybrid:** An integration of multiple cloud models (private, public, community) was provided where those cloud renters maintain uniqueness while forming one unit. Universal, ubiquitous protocols are given to access data for presentation.

To consume a service, a cloud supplier and a cloud customer each needs to expand trust beyond their own IT resources, past the demarcation service access point between the cloud customer along with other cloud actors. A cloud user is responsible for the execution of their safety and privacy controls demanded on its side, but is dependent on the support implemented from other cloud actors.

A number of the privacy and security controls achieved by cloud users are inherited from the other cloud actors. Therefore, a cloud customer entrusts the cloud provider and affiliated actors with implementing the safety measures required to protect the cloud customer's data and also to meet the service agreement and the service level agreement, if they exist. Assessing all system components, deciphering the intricacy of this complex ecosystem, identifying the logical boundary of trusted elements that service the cloud-based information system and constitute the cloud ecosystem—the trust boundary, and finally building a trust relationship among cloud actors is essential for cloud consumers and for the successful set up and operations of their cloud-based information system.

A trust boundary is your logical perimeter that typically spans beyond physical limits to represent the extent to which cloud-based IT resources inside an established cloud ecosystem are trusted (see Figure 5.9 to get a graphical representation of the concept). This extended trust boundary encompasses the resources out of all cloud actors and explains a logical lively border of this cloud-based information system and the supporting subsystems, viewed from the cloud customer's perspective.

The confidence boundary is elastic and adjusts into the cloud ecosystem's dynamic modifications triggered by provisioning or decommissioning of their resources, and by information securely resting or travelling. To construct and maintain trust from the cloud ecosystem, cloud consumers need to have the ability to inspect the security controls deployed inside this border and determine the business's risk tolerance to this confidentiality, integrity and availability risks resulting from working on this cloud-based information system.

The most normal method to set up an agreement with a cloud supplier is via service agreements and service level agreements that describe security requirements, capacities, and agreed-upon standards, policies, and methods of trust execution (such as monitoring and auditing).

Figure 5.9 depicts the trust boundary as the surface of the bounds. By way of example, building confidence and identifying the trust border in an IaaS cloud ecosystem means setting the procedure for creating trusted platforms and aggregating them into reputable pools of resources at design time. At runtime, trust boundaries become elastic and dynamically adjust as the multitenancy, and resource pooling features of the cloud are displayed. By way of example, a burst out to a shadow from on-premises resources requires that the trust border dynamically re-shapes to pay out the bursting cloud infrastructure, and therefore this infrastructure needs to be trusted.

At the opposite end, the users accessing the cloud resources will need to be reliable, so the supporting authentication and access control mechanisms and the networking that connects them to the tools will need to be dependable. In this scenario, trusted means the level of assurance was established, and the safety position of the elements was assessed, along with the residual risk gauged for all aspects of the processing based on the sensitivity of this information at the user-data border.

At runtime, auditing and logging demand to encourage assurance mechanics that all essential aspects of the trust bonds are present for workload processing and therefore are fulfilling data confidentiality, integrity, and accessibility requirements.

Continuous monitoring may be necessary for the condition of the safety program and functions as a significant portion of the risk management procedure. Even the organization's overall security structure and accompanying security policies and controls are monitored to make sure that organization-wide operations stay within an acceptable amount of risk, considering any changes that occur.

5.7. DEFINING YOUR ROOT OF TRUST

Trust is an intransitive relation with a specific hierarchy. What that means is that trust flows down a chain until it reaches the root of confidence. Cloud implementations have several layers of abstraction, from hardware to virtualization to guest operating systems.

The security and privacy of the user's data depend on the integrity and trustworthiness of the cloud ecosystem, which depends on the accumulative trustworthiness of those layers that may potentially compromise or manipulate data integrity or confidentiality.

The trustworthiness of each layer relies on the hardware or applications protected modules (HSM/SSM) that are inherently trusted and that perform the cryptographic functions engineered to secure the data and the operations of every layer of the cloud stack.

Recognizing who owns the root of trust is a foundational element to the architecture of an information system. Roots of trust are not just the inherent anchors for many calculated components that support protected operations of the cloud ecosystem, but they will need to get trusted by the cloud actors in order to assess the integrity and trustworthiness of their cloud ecosystem, to identify the trust border, and also to build the necessary trust connection among cloud actors. In a data-centric architecture, it is essential that the cloud user owns the origin of confidence as it pertains to the cloud customer's user information and associated user-data border. This means that a cloud user should have the cryptographic keys used by the HSM/SSM that is securing the cloud layers (storage, hypervisors, virtual machines [VM], applications, and user data at rent, in transit and memory).

The cloud consumer should have the key used to secure the lowest common denominator of the cloud ecosystem depending on the sensitivity of the information housed therein. Information systems containing nonsensitive data may have to have the cloud provider encrypted. Information systems comprising more sensitive data may need VM or storage encryption, where the cloud user owns the key along with the VM or room being unlocked with a hardware or software security device. Cloud access security agents serve to encrypt data in transit and at rest inside cloud providers, ensuring that cloud customers' data remains encrypted as it traverses the cloud ecosystem. Defining a root of confidence is a crucial element of cloud design, and needs to be ascertained before issuing a security authorization for the information system.

5.8. MANAGING USER AUTHENTICATION AND AUTHORIZATION

Understanding and defining user authentication and authorization among cloud actors is another crucial element of cloud design. Without knowing who is logging into the cloud-based data system, and who is accessing what data, cloud actors are unable to guard the data housed by a cloud ecosystem.

Understanding who the consumers are, what evidence on who is attempting to access, where the data are saved, and how consumers are trying to access these data—all these are crucial pieces of information which help cloud consumers determine a proper cloud structure and deployment model. User authentication is the process of establishing confidence in the identity of a user, typically using a valid username and a valid token (password, essential, and biometrics data) to grant access to a specific information system(s) or assets. A credential is an object or data structure that authoritatively binds an identity (and optionally, additional features) into a token possessed and controlled by the consumer.

By way of example, a username and password set is a data structure or a credential. If the provided credential matches the information in the authentication database, then the user is allowed access to this information system. If the credential does not match, the authentication fails and access is denied.

The kind of credential used should be commensurate with the level of assurance defined by the sensitivity of the cloud consumer's user information. By leveraging data, user, and location, a varying degree of the certificate can be used if some of the variables as mentioned above change. By way of example, if a cloud user is currently in the United States and accesses a cloud information system typically using a web browser on his or her personal computer, the user would be prompted to enter the password and username to access stated system. In the background, the data system may verify additional information collected from the user's device, including geolocation, IP address, and so on.

When the same cloud user travels globally and gets the cloud information system via a web browser on a computer, the cloud information program's authentication server may identify another IP address or a different geolocation. After this new information is collected from the user's device, the system can prompt the user to supply additional credentials for a higher degree of assurance when supporting the identity of the user before granting said access. User consent is the process of enforcing policies such as determining what services or resources a user is permitted to access.

Typically, user authorization occurs within the context of authentication. After a user is authenticated, he or she might be licensed to access different components of a cloud information system. Ensuring that consumer authorization is applied to the lowest common denominator of every element of a cloud ecosystem is vital for ensuring the security of the information stored inside the cloud data system.

Granting users more power than they are authorized to use can undermine a system. What is more, protecting user credentials to safeguard against tampering or abuse is critical and needs to be part of the security policies employed within the safety authorization program of their cloud-based information platform. The authorities can be instrumental in granting or withholding user authentication and authorization to the server.

The cloud ecosystem architecture will probably dictate which cloud celebrity is responsible for handling the server and also for authenticating and authorizing users. Cloud users are required to select the best fitting solution for their cloud-based information system, since the user authentication and authorization procedures (high level, general perspective of the identified tasks), policies (a principle or law that drives the processes and procedures) and procedures (detailed steps required to execute an action or a job within a method) are instrumental in safeguarding their information in a cloud ecosystem. However, for cloud customers to take full advantage of cloud computing economies of scale, it is essential to build the necessary level of confidence and gain visibility for the service. This ought to fully leverage the cutting-edge technologies embedded into cloud suppliers' and cloud specialized agents' supplies, and provision resources quickly and elastically in a way commensurate with the pace and dynamic changes of the business.

Table 5.1. Cloud actors definitions

Actor	Definition
Cloud Consumer	A person or organization that maintains a business relationship with, and uses service from, cloud providers.
Cloud Provider	A person, organization, or entity responsible for making a service available to interested parties.
Cloud Auditor	A party that can conduct an independent assessment of cloud services, information system operations, performance, and security of the cloud implementation.
Cloud Broker	An entity that manages the use, performance, and delivery of cloud services and negotiates relationships between cloud providers and cloud consumers.
Cloud Carrier	An intermediary that provides connectivity and transport of cloud services from cloud providers to cloud consumers.

REFERENCES

NIST. December, 2011a. "Guidelines on Security and Privacy in Public Cloud Computing," Special Publication 800-144.

NIST. September, 2011b. "NIST Cloud Computing Reference Architecture," Special Publication 500-292. http://www.nist.gov/customcf/get_pdf.cfm?pub_id=909505

NIST. September, 2011c. "The NIST Definition of Cloud Computing," Special Publication 800-145. http://csrc.nist.gov/publications/PubsSPs.html#800-145

NIST. May, 2013. "NIST Cloud Computing Security Reference Architecture," Special Publication 500-299 (draft).

NIST. n.d. "Cloud Computing Security Essentials and Architecture." http://ws680.nist.gov/publication/get_pdf.cfm?pub_id=919233

Microsoft. 2016. "Cloud Computing: What Is Infrastructure as a Service." https://technet.microsoft.com/en-us/library/hh509051.aspx

CHAPTER 6

CLOUD SECURITY

6.1. THE STATE OF CLOUD SECURITY

The Continuing Fiscal crisis and the rising computational and storage demands have imposed significant modifications on modern IT infrastructure.

IT cost reduction has been accomplished by offloading information and computations to computing. Even though this financial model has discovered flexible ground bringing in investments, lots of people and businesses are hesitant to utilize cloud solutions due to the many safety, privacy, and trust problems that have emerged. Nearly all security specialists believed that cloud computing problems ought to be solved using existing countermeasures inherited from traditional IT systems as well as dispersed systems which are the ancestors of cloud computing environments. It did not take long for them to understand this original approach was incorrect, due to the principal qualities of the cloud computing version, specifically:

a. **Scale:** In order to realize substantial economies, the cloud version supports enormous concentrations of hardware tools to supply to the services that are supported, and

b. **Architecture:** Even though clients who discuss hardware and software resources are usually unrelated, they rely upon logical isolation mechanisms to guard their data. This trend toward international supply and redundancy implies that tools are often managed in the majority, both logically and physically (ENISA 2009).

Both these attributes of cloud computing systems are in the core of the cloud safety, privacy, and trust problems that have emerged. Considering scale, the very first attribute analyzed, cloud computing infrastructures have attained massive levels of computational tools. Consequently, in the event of a practical threat scenario, the effect will be more significant than what happens in usual IT and dispersed systems, affecting significantly greater numbers of infrastructures, services, and people using them. Because of this, we state that combined with scaling resources we have fulfilled safely, privacy, but trust problems in cloud computing methods still remain.

The next attribute of cloud computing is structure. Cloud computing methods guarantee logical and physical isolation for their clients as they generally share physical tools when they utilize the exact same cloud support. However, physical isolation is quite tricky when they discuss the computational tools of the same physical machine, possibly using cloud solutions or virtual machines (VMs). Thus, most cloud providers (CPs) attempt to provide plausible isolation to their clients, which can be more feasible. In this scenario there are privacy, security, and trust problems that cannot be solved in traditional ways. Because of this, new countermeasures are needed in these instances. In accordance with ISO 27001, a hazard is a possible event. When a hazard turns into a real occasion, it might result in an undesirable incident. It is undesirable because the episode may damage a company or a method, resulting in a safety incident and/or the breach of consumers' privacy.

The classification method, introduced in this chapter, utilizes three different categories: dangers linked to the infrastructure, dangers linked to the service supplier, and generic dangers. The important objective of this proposed classification is to decrease the load on the cloud administrators in security-related problems, by pointing out the significant issues that arise and thus saving them money and time. To be able to attain the objective of producing a proper classification, it is crucial to offer the proper information to comprehend the dangers that came along with the emerging technologies of cloud computing methods. After introducing the suggested classification via a thorough description of these identified risks against cloud surroundings, we will offer an overall picture of the dangers identified in each class, in addition to advice on countermeasures that may be available for discovering and preventing each hazard.

6.2. UNDERSTANDING THE THREATS

Prior to introducing the danger classification, it is very important to understand their uniqueness against new dangers encountered in traditional IT systems or distributed systems. To be able to make our work easy, we will use information given by two safety organizations, the people of ENISA

(2009) along with the Cloud Security Alliance (2011). A number of years ago ENISA introduced a questionnaire titled *Safety in cloud computing methods*. This survey starts by assessing the advantages of cloud computing methods. But, though there are advantages concerning scale and source concentration, with regard to the very best security dangers, it is apparent that the advantages are outnumbered. The same survey classifies dangers, dividing them into organizational and policy dangers, technical threats, legal threats, and dangers not particular to the cloud. Every hazard is assigned a tier that changes from low to high and can be described based on its likelihood, influence, vulnerabilities, and influenced assets.

It has to be stressed that the non-cloud-specific risks comprise just one class and therefore are fewer than the others. Because of this, the manifestation of cloud computing methods has attracted an entirely new collection of security threats which were previously unknown. A collection of security threats describes the shortage of isolation which is an Economical Denial of Sustainability (EDoS), it describes fatigue of computational tools of a cloud system in a client function. Another noteworthy case is that of malicious software—a theory redefined in the context of cloud computing methods and showing once more that there are fewer vulnerabilities which are not cloud-specific than those created by the cloud systems.

The Cloud Security Alliance affirms that, regardless of the similarities in safety controls between IT and cloud technologies, there are many differences between the two in the dangers to which a company might be exposed. CPs use operational versions and the technology behind these could be where the new dangers emerge from. There may be gaps in the safety responsibilities of the supplier and the customer among the cloud support versions. Additionally, as the goal of the CPs is price efficacy, thus attaining scale, reuse, and standardization, they arrive at a point at which security mechanisms lose their versatility.

ENISA and the Cloud Security Alliance deal with clients and secure users of cloud systems who might grow into the biggest dangers together with customers with increased privileges. When compared with conventional IT solutions, assaults on the cloud surface have enlarged, not just due to their shared assets but also on account of the additional attack vectors that an adversary may use for exploiting a possible vulnerability in the VM, at the cloud control system, or at any other element of this cloud infrastructure.

Based on Xiao and Xiao (2012), the expression insider, to get an information platform, applies to anybody with accepted access, freedom, or understanding of the data system and its services and assignments. A malicious insider is someone moved to negatively affect a company's mission through a variety of activities that undermine information confidentiality, ethics, and accessibility, taking benefit of their privileges. Similarly, for cloud computing, an insider is regarded as an entity that:

- Works on your cloud server
- Has privileged entry into the cloud tools
- Uses the cloud hosting solutions

Thus, cloud insiders (Figure 6.1) are primarily privileged users, who might be prompted to undermine the safety of their cloud infrastructure. Their activities might bring about a temporary break, as the breach of valid users' privacy, or perhaps the permanent disruption of the supplied services, based on their rights. It is highlighted that VM-related info, like the construction of the digital system being put up for its internal communication to one of the supplied VMs, maybe just expressed by privileged users and manipulated through the subsequent steps of an assault. To attain this, a malicious user might attempt to map all available VMs and to extract additional VM-related data (Xiao and Xiao 2012), to conquer cloud safety or to violate users' privacy.

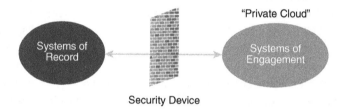

Figure 6.1. Cloud insiders are primarily privileged users, who might be prompted to undermine the safety of their cloud infrastructure

6.3. CLASSIFICATION AND COUNTERMEASURES

To ease the investigation of the security threats faced by cloud technologies, it is required to classify the known dangers (ENISA 2009) into different categories. Our suggestion for this type of classification uses three main classes:

- Infrastructure and server related dangers, which influence the whole cloud infrastructure.
- Service provider—associated dangers that might influence the consumers that seek an agency in the cloud.
- Common dangers that may affect the infrastructure and the support providers or customers.

It is vital to stress that for the remainder of this chapter all the references to hazard assessment tools do not signify a countermeasure; instead, a particular process might be employed to recognize the right countermeasures for each hazard.

6.3.1. RECRUITMENT AND HOST THREATS

All dangers in cloud technologies may be related to the whole cloud infrastructure or they may be cloud-specific. In both instances, their significance is high. Because of this, they could have catastrophic results on the system as also on the life of an individual. This kind of unauthorized physical access can endanger the system's apparatus and equipment, and may result in denial of service (DoS) for a lengthy period. Risk evaluation tools, such as CRAMM and Octave (Caralli et al. 2002; Yazar 2002), can avert such issues and have to be considered during the first phase of the cloud system's growth (ENISA 2009).

On several occasions, workers pose a severe danger to the cloud system. Deficient training or neglect is closely linked to inconsistent and irregular activities of the ordinary worker. Such activities might involve the unintentional loss or deletion of their backup info and operational or security logs.

A risk management strategy in combination with the evolution of an exhaustive safety policy can lead to the prevention of similar events. These steps help the workers to adhere to a routine for processes, significantly reducing the probability of causing crucial and unrecoverable errors.

There is no limitation to exploiting information located in the garbage. Sometimes data extracted in the garbage can be valuable for somebody who plans to assault the cloud system. Information leaks may also be exploited by malicious users hoping to establish social engineering attacks or alleviate more threatening situations. Each organization has to adopt/ establish policies concerning the life cycle and also the security of sensitive data and should guarantee that the policies are followed closely by the workers without exclusion (Krutz and Vines 2010).

This type of attack demands several efforts (brute force attack), and so it is pretty easy to stop by limiting invalid password attempts (Krutz and Vines 2010).

During a social engineering attack, the attacker may gain access by merely eliciting the essential information, like customers' credentials. Otherwise, privilege escalation techniques can offer the malicious user all the necessary clearance to get these data. A good illustration of this predicament is the SYSRET exploit, where malicious third parties reaped the benefits of AMD's SYSRET education when put on Intel platforms (Dunlap 2014). To be able to prevent such situations, it is very important to use current and appropriate safety countermeasures and rigorous access control (ENISA 2009).

These logs, which are primarily used by system administrators and auditors, supply crucial pieces of info that malicious parties may use to launch strikes. In addition, these logs may expose the identity of their users as they contain sensitive and personal data. Security of safety logs has to be a topic of high importance because once exposed, they may jeopardize the whole information system and its customers (ENISA 2009; Saripalli and Walters 2010; Subashini and Kavitha 2011).

6.3.2. NETWORK BREAKS

Each data system and notably a cloud infrastructure offers access to its services via distinct networks. Malicious users can benefit from those vulnerabilities by compromising the safety of their community or by preventing its appropriate functioning. These network fractures can pose a severe threat to the functioning of CPs.

Thousands of clients might be impacted at precisely the same time along with the CP and will end up as being untrustworthy to the present and to potential new clients (ENISA 2009; Ritchey and Ammann 2000). Most operating systems do not completely delete the information while, in a different scenario, timely information deletion might be unavailable. A CP might want to apply several alterations to its structure, like altering the location of this machine, building a hardware reallocation, as well as replacing hardware. During these modifications, because of technical reasons, the information may not be moved or appropriately destroyed, leaving them vulnerable.

People frequently install malware which collects data for mapping the cloud network. When an individual understands his present position either in the system or the physical machine of this cloud infrastructure, he may use it to enhance his rights and to gain access to additional VMs. When this happens, the malicious user may retrieve information he otherwise would not have been permitted to get (Ristenpart et al. 2009).

On the flip side, it is a frequent occurrence that several cloud systems do not correctly implement the encryption or cryptographic protocols, even in the worst case scenario where encryption does not exist in any way. Therefore, a comprehensive implementation of modern cryptographic techniques should always be a top priority because it can shield the machine from numerous malicious functions (Grobauer, Walloshek, and Stöcker 2011). It is a new threat that has emerged in cloud computing environments. The most significant situations are:

- Identity theft: An attacker can steal the accounts and the tools of a client to utilize them to their advantage. In a situation like this, the attacker may get free access to providers whereas the victim's account is billed for these services. Additionally, the attacker could use the stolen identity, and by behaving maliciously, he might endanger the victim's reputation.
- The cloud client might have no practical limitations on the usage of resources that are paid. Consequently, he might impose sudden loads on such resources.
- An attacker can use a public station to use the clients' metered resources.

In these types of situations, services might not be accessible to clients and access control might be compromised. Along with this, the trustworthiness of this CP is threatened. Kaliski and Pauley indicate risk assessment as a means to prevent EDoS (Kaliski and Pauley 2010). The term "isolation" describes security and performance isolation. Because of this, the implementation of a single service should not interfere with the next. Typically, isolation could be accomplished by only using different physical servers or remote system infrastructures. However, with regard to cloud computing, it is quite hard to have complete isolation, as the VMs discuss sources. Because of this, in the event of isolation malfunction, somebody who has access to shared resources is going to have the ability to recover confidential data (ENISA 2009; Raj et al. 2009). Cloud solutions possess a metering capability with an abstraction level right to this service type, such as processing and storage. The metering information is utilized for service delivery and charging service (Grobauer, Walloshek, and Stöcker 2011). An approach was suggested by Widder et al. which indicated the usage of an intricate event-processing motor (Widder et al. 2007).

6.3.3. LOCK-IN

Many problems happen when the cloud infrastructure changes in possession and coverage, while the prior customers stay as clients. A difficulty of major significance appears when clients cannot transfer their information from one CP to another. In this scenario, we can have many different lock-in issues based upon the structure of this cloud system. It is very difficult to extract the information from every customer because of legal or technical factors. In the case of the SaaS structure, the issue of provider's lock-in could take place. The issue in the PaaS structure could be about the API coating because CPs do not utilize precisely the same virtualization platform. Clients should check if the new provider employs the very same platforms or compatible ones. IaaS lock-in fluctuates on the basis of the infrastructure used by each client. To be able to prevent this from happening, the right CP has to be selected after extensive research, and particular attention has to be paid to any alteration in the cloud coverage (ENISA 2009; Widjaya 2011).

6.4. COMPLIANCE ISSUES

Businesses and organizations migrate to cloud systems for many reasons. Since these businesses have been using security certifications and other criteria before the migration, compliance issues may emerge.

This is principal since the CP might not use the same safety criteria or standards, or perhaps because the safety schemes might not be harmonious with one another. It is thus essential for the clients to assess if the CP can provide services that are harmonious with their deployments and can host solutions following their requirements. Otherwise, this can cause DoS for a lengthy period, while the consumers' disappointment will sabotage the operator's standing (ENISA 2009). As cloud systems might possess different elements of the infrastructure spread through various countries, this danger gets much worse.

Contemplating these problems, it may be concluded that there are many open challenges regarding data provenance. This leads to doubt for the cloud clients, who should be aware of the provenance of the information they are using. Each CP needs to form its provenance system, to ensure the quality of the supplied services and safeguard data confidentiality and customers' privacy.

If these conditions are compromised, authority problems might be raised regarding the information and their storage (ENISA 2009; Vouk 2008).

6.5. INFRASTRUCTURE MODIFICATIONS

As technology grows, better hardware and software alternatives are introduced. CPs may upgrade or update their software and equipment. This could lead to additional fees for every client, even when the latter continues to utilize the same amount of resources throughout the cloud. What is more, the intellectual property of this saved/traded data might be in danger, if the proper security mechanisms do not adequately protect data. CPs should pay attention to such things and put in extraordinary efforts to come up with rigorous rules and safety policies regarding the correct use of their systems, to prevent legal troubles.

6.6. DATA PROCESSING

Along with information provenance, another significant concern in cloud computing is information processing. A customer cannot be specific about how the cloud system will manipulate his information and also if the processing complies with all the legal framework of the nation where he resides. Many CPs describe the processes they follow along with the certificates they might have, but if the data are protected against malicious users, it cannot be guaranteed whether the consumers' stored information has been legally accessed or not. This raises another dilemma: how can these data be assessed from the legal standpoint and (at precisely the same time) be shielded from disclosure, without breaking users' privacy (ENISA 2009)?

6.7. ADMINISTRATIVE AND ASSETS

It is likely that a CP will alter its administrative employees (e.g., system or network administrators) or the entire cloud system might even be sold to another provider. This can result in many safety issues because the new owners might not always fulfill the safety demands of the prior owner/ administrator. This might have impact on the confidentiality of the information, availability, and integrity, and hence on the CP's reputation. Therefore, it is crucial to keep the previously established safety measures for a period before the new management decides to change them.

6.8. DOS

DoS to cotenants because of misjudgment or even misallocation of resources considering that cloud methods offer resource sharing can result in malicious actions carried out by a single tenant affecting another. What is more, a client might not have the ability to access a particular service since some other person might have booked the accessible resources. This can turn into a significant problem as it considerably degrades the provider's standing on account of the clients' dissatisfaction (they cannot have access to the services that they cover). Therefore, CPs will consider and maintain the client's right to get the reserved services (ENISA 2009). The centralization of storage and also shared tenancy of physical hardware puts at risk the information of several customers because the disclosure of personal data is not considered a criminal activity in all countries. It is thus tough for every agency of every country to take particular care of each cloud system hosted under their jurisdiction. Consequently, clients should consider the legal framework of this CP to steer clear of privacy-related problems.

6.9. SERVICE PROVIDER

Another group that has emerged in cloud technologies are the providers of the service supplier threats and are distinguished from the other two groups by the fact that clients looking for cloud support are influenced. Although in the long run the whole infrastructure could be damaged by these dangers, the clients are the first to confront these issues. In cases like this, an attacker intercepts and conserves the messages that are transmitted. After spoofing those messages, the attacker then resends them into the ceremony, impersonating the communication participants. Additional countermeasures might contain a time stamp, which suggests the time that the message has been delivered (Kennedy 2015).

6.10. INFORMATION INTERCEPTION

This is a set of strikes inherited from conventional IT systems. As cloud systems are more scalable, the consequences of these attacks can also be scalable and in the majority of instances more severe. This group of strikes comprises

Man-in-the-middle: In this kind of attack, the attacker may impersonate the victim by altering the public key/user association. Because of this, the sender encrypts the message with the attacker's public key; consequently, the latter could get, intercept, and alter the message. Last, the attacker encrypts the forged message together with the true sufferer's public key and forwards it to the sufferer (Kennedy 2015). Their objective is to acquire information or to make a base for a subsequent attack.

CPs do not create browsers that are appropriately safe for this function. Consequently, computer users utilize many different browsers with safety attributes that mostly depend on their applications version. Thus, every time a security violation or exploit emerges in a particular browser, it will influence the entire cloud infrastructure (Jensen et al. 2009).

It was just a concept until 2008, as it had been found that Amazon's EC2 solutions were vulnerable to wrapping attacks. The particular vulnerability was a soap structure manipulation which was utilized along with this technique. This group of strikes cannot be readily detected, and it remains a great danger for the cloud (Gruschka and Lo Iaocono 2009; Jensen et al. 2009). This type of manipulation may induce the translation and consequently the implementation of the prohibited code. Considering these attacks are extremely common, and in most cases readily exploitable, cloud suppliers should consider deploying countermeasures and security schemes from the very first phases of their institution (Grobauer, Walloshek, and Stöcker 2011).

6.11. CLIENTS' NEGLIGENCE AND CLOUD SECURITY

Cloud clients fail to properly secure their cloud computing surroundings, allowing malicious users to assault the cloud system. Clients must recognize they have to guard their information and resources. Sometimes, cloud clients erroneously assume that the supplier is responsible for guaranteeing the safety of the information. This type of threat cannot be addressed via auditing or alternative practices. Each corporation should always keep a high safety standard even when the clients do not comply with the right processes (ENISA 2009).

One step in the right direction is by including customer interfaces that command lots of VMs and also strengthening the operation of the general cloud system (ENISA 2009). Regular browser upgrades and setup of various types of IDS in several VMs, as Cheng et al., imply, can lessen this danger (Cheng, Roschke, and Meinel 2009; Roschke, Cheng, and Meinel 2009, 2010).

6.12. REDUCTION OF GOVERNANCE

As previously mentioned, the safety methods that cloud clients use considerably deviate from the instructions of their CPs. This type of contradiction can lead to a reduction of control and governance that could have a detrimental influence on the cloud system and naturally on its data. With this end in mind, each CP should continue to keep its clients up to date with both transparent and rigorous security procedures and instructions while, in cases of outsourcing, the spouses' service has to be harmonious with these instructions/policies (ENISA 2009).

6.13. COMMON RISKS

Here is the previous threat category. It is a set of dangers that may affect the infrastructure and the support providers/customers. In the event of a security violation, the cloud surroundings face significant impact.

An attacker may impersonate (e.g., via a telephone call or e-mail) a manager, a chief technician, or other essential entities to elicit confidential information which may be used for attacking the machine indirectly or directly. Such advice might contain passwords, media topologies, used software and hypervisor variant along with many others, which may offer the attacker the proper knowledge to establish an assault. Social engineering may be mitigated through rigorous procedures and naturally by auditing, which plays an integral part in preventing such strikes (Cloud Security Alliance 2010; Orgill et al. 2004).

The danger from other strikes is its ability (a) to set up its weapons in a "dispersed" way across the web and (b) to aggregate those forces to create traffic that is overwhelming. Distributed denial of service (DdoS) attacks are becoming stronger since attackers have taken advantage of this cloud architecture that has inherited the benefits and disadvantages of distributed systems (Bakshi and Yogesh 2010). However, a solution suggested by Bakshi and Yogesh indicates the execution of an intrusion detection system (IDS) to a VM (Douligeris and Mitrokotsa 2004).

6.14. ENCRYPTION KEYS

Vulnerability or reduction within this kind of assault, worker negligence, or absence of safety policies creates the essential keys (document encryption, SSL, client personal keys) vulnerable to malicious users that are neither licensed nor authenticated to utilize them (ENISA 2009). Such collapse may offer access to unauthorized users who might launch strikes against the cloud infrastructure along with other clients.

6.15. SERVICE ENGINE PRESENCE

The support engine has been designed and supported by the cloud system vendors and, sometimes from the open source community. The service engine is more prone to strikes or sudden failure; this implies it may be exposed to different malicious surgeries. For example, an attacker may control the support engine and gain access to the information contained within the client environment (Kennedy 2015). Regular security upgrades of this service engine will have the ability to partly address the issue.

Some kinds of malware have been programmed to open individual ports to allow access by attackers or for potential manipulation of the program's vulnerabilities (Krutz and Vines 2010). Because malware rises and progresses each day, addressing it is not a trivial endeavor.

This produces a malicious partitioning which is one of the worst threats against data systems and cloud computing systems because cloud architectures demand specific functions such as system administrators and auditors, managed security service providers, and so on, who are regarded as quite insecure (ENISA 2009).

An advice on whether the particular hazard can be addressed through some technical countermeasures (technical option) or via some organizational or procedural countermeasures (non-toxic alternative) can be made based on whether a threat is coated (•), partly coated (○), or not insured (–).

Generally speaking, it is the procedure for recognition of a thing's identity and the confidence in its behavior. From the cloud perspective, the expression thing involves the CP along with his employees, the cloud client along with the information owner. Trust can be accomplished through trust mechanics that use trust models. A trust model is a control technique or protocol which includes trust institution, confidence renewal, and hope withdrawal. Trust direction of cloud computing methods cannot be performed together with the traditional trust models. This is a result of the distinctive qualities of the cloud technologies—that is, their dimensions, location, the absence of perimeter, number of consumers, and lack of assurance—which names the present trust models for dispersed systems improper. Among the most critical barriers to the widespread installation of cloud systems is the dilemma of confidence between the consumer and the CP. When data are saved on the cloud, users believe they are losing control, and they are suspicious about topics such as who has access to this, how is their information processed or/and replicated, and so on. The trust mechanisms which may be implemented act as countermeasures to the prior concerns, because trust achieves to set entities' relationship safely and quickly. However, existing trust models used, for example, to get a data center that is limited from the perimeter of a company, are not suitable for cloud computing environments. The main reasons for this are listed below:

- **Information processing:** When a client transfers his information to the cloud, the central processor of this information is not the real owner any longer, but the supplier. This simple fact makes things different concerning trust because a brand new threat parameter has been increased. To put it differently, the physical chip of this information should always be wholly trustworthy. On the other hand, the CP cannot be entirely reliable.

- **Information place:** In traditional methods, the geolocation of information is always understood. When deploying solutions in cloud computing methods, the physical location of information is no longer understood or entirely reliable. A trust model that does not consider the location of information in transit cannot be regarded as necessary in cloud technologies.
- **Information accessibility:** The place from where users get the information, that is, the cloud is unknown and cannot be localized.
- **Number of consumers:** In traditional systems, it is not tough to specify the number of individuals who may access the machine. But here only a client pays for a service and the supplier of the particular service pays the other supplier for part of the service he is assumed to be providing to the client.

There are numerous cloud-specific trust models indicated in the literature. However, these versions should be assessed via a listing of prerequisites which a trust model for cloud surroundings should meet.

- **Trust metric:** At a trust model, it is required to specify a way of measuring confidence. Since trust is an abstract expression, a way of quantifying the confidence value of a cloud supplier or a cloud client has to be defined. It is also required to specify the measured levels of confidence for part of the confidence model.
- **Abnormal behavior:** A significant element in the evaluation of trust ought to be the strange behavior of consumers from the cloud. A behavior that deviates from the typical or an outdated behavioral background or possibly short-term accessibility should lead to zero hope. Because of this, it is deemed essential for cloud assurance models to specify which behavior is labeled as ordinary and which is not. What is more, the weights and standards (time, background, weights of ordinary versus abnormal) must also be clarified.
- **Identity management/authentication:** To be able to accumulate confidence related opinions, a model should be confident that the identities of those users are real.
- **Data safety:** Trust management and applicable models are employed as part of the total security management strategy of this cloud. A trust model must define the minimum prerequisites for attaining an acceptable degree of information security. The SLA ought to be a part of this trust management procedure.

Cloud computing has been among the most well-known technologies in information and communications technology (ICT) in the past couple of decades. Among the chief obstacles in its adoption is the sense of bitterness because of the breach of privacy. Excluded from the constraints of present day classifications of dangers for cloud systems, which consider the significant cloud dependencies or use risk assessment tools, this chapter introduces an alternate classification in which the dangers are segregated into three classes.

The first class comprises the dangers against the infrastructure which includes the server of a cloud system. The next category is about the dangers impacting the service suppliers, and the last one includes other generic safety hazards. The goal of the suggested classification is to make an extremely efficient safety record for cloud systems which will be helpful to everybody who wants to construct or utilize a cloud infrastructure/service. What is more, fine-tuned trust direction could be a fantastic substitute for several security risks. The principal reason is that following the use of a fantastic trust control mechanism, users can decide on the supplier according to their needs and trustworthiness and suppliers can refuse or accept consumers based on how trusted those are. It is thus essential to create cloud-specific trust versions that encourage trust metrics and also take into consideration behavioral user information, quality of support, and geolocation of the user's terminal.

REFERENCES

Bakshi, A., and B. Yogesh. 2010. Securing Cloud from DDOS Attacks Using Intrusion Detection System in Virtual Machine. *ICCSN '10 Proceeding of the 2010 Second International Conference on Communication Software and Networks*, February 26–28, pp. 260–264. Washington, DC: IEEE Computer Society.

Caralli, R.A., J.F. Stevens, L.R. Young, and W.R. Wilson. 2002. "Introducing OCTAVE Allegro: Improving the Information Security Risk Assessment Process," *Software Engineering Institute*.

Cheng, F., S. Roschke, and C. Meinel. 2009. "Implementing IDS Management on Lock-keeper." In *Information Security Practice and Experience*, eds. F. Bao, H. Li, and G. Wang. Berlin, Germany: Springer, pp. 360–71.

Cloud Security Alliance. 2010. "CloudAudit." https://cloudsecurityalliance.org/articles/cloud-security-alliance-announces-that-cloudaudit-has-become-an-official-project-of-the-csa/

Cloud Security Alliance. 2011. "Security Guidance for Critical Areas of Focus in Cloud Computing V3. 0."

Douligeris, C., and A. Mitrokotsa. 2004. "DDoS Attacks and Defense Mechanisms: Classification and State-of-threat." *Computer Networks* no. 5, pp. 643–666, 2004.

Dunlap, G. 2014. "Sysret, Xen Project, A Linux Foundation Collaborative Project." https://www.xenproject.org/about/in-the-news/146-xen-to-become-linux-foundation-collaborative-project.html

ENISA. 2009. "Cloud Computing—Benefits, Risks and Recommendations for Information Security," *European Network and Information Security Agency.*

Grobauer, B., T. Walloshek, and E. Stöcker. 2011. "Understanding Cloud Computing Vulnerabilities." *IEEE Security and Privacy* 9, no. 2, pp. 50–57.

Gruschka, N., and L. Lo Iaocono. 2009. Vulnerable Cloud: SOAP Message Security Validation Revisited. *Proceedings of the International Conference on Web Services*, July. Los Angeles, CA: IEEE.

Kaliski, B.S., Jr., and W. Pauley. 2010. Toward Risk Assessment as a Service in Cloud Environments. *Proceedings of the 2nd USENIX Conference on Hot Topics in Cloud Computing*, June 22–25, p. 13. Berkeley, CA: USENIX Association.

Kennedy, D. 2015. "The Social-Engineer Toolkit (SET)," *TrustedSec.* https://github.com/trustedsec/social-engineer-toolkit

Krutz, R.L., and R.D. Vines. 2010. *Cloud Security: A Comprehensive Guide to Secure Cloud Computing*. Indianapolis, IN: Wiley.

Orgill, G.L., G.W. Romney, M.G. Bailey, and P.M. Orgill. 2004. The Urgency for Effective User Privacy-education to Counter Social Engineering Attacks on Secure Computer Systems. *Proceedings of the Conference on Information Technology Education,* October 28–30, pp. 177–181. New York, NY: CITC5.

Raj, H., R. Nathuji, A. Singh, and P. England. 2009. Resource Management for Isolation Enhanced Cloud Services. *Proceedings of the Workshop on Cloud Computing Security*, pp. 77–84. Chicago, IL: ACM.

Ristenpart, T., E. Tromer, H. Shacham, and S. Savage. 2009. Hey, You, Get of My Cloud: Exploring Information Leakage in Third-party Compute Clouds. *Proceedings of the Conference on Computer and Communications Security*, November 9–13. Chicago, IL: ACM.

Ritchey, R.W., and P. Ammann. 2000. Using Model Checking to Analyze Network Vulnerabilities. *Proceedings in Security and Privacy*, pp. 156–165. Berkeley, CA: IEEE.

Roschke S., F. Cheng, and C. Meinel. 2009. Intrusion Detection in the Cloud, DASC'09. *Eighth IEEE International Conference on Dependable, Autonomic and Secure Computing*, December 12–14, pp. 729–734. Chengdu, China: IEEE.

Roschke, S., F. Cheng, and C. Meinel. 2010. "An Advanced IDS Management Architecture." *Journal of Information Assurance and Security* 5, pp. 246–55.

Saripalli, P., and B. Walters. 2010. QUIRC: A Quantitative Impact and Risk Assessment Framework for Cloud Security. *IEEE 3rd International Conference on Cloud Computing*, July 5–10, Miami, FL.

Subashini, S., and V. Kavitha. 2011. "A Survey on Security Issues in Service Delivery Models of Cloud Computing." *Journal of Network and Computer Applications* 34, no. 1, pp. 1–11.

Vouk, M.A. 2008. Cloud Computing—Issues, Research and Implementation. *Proceedings of the International Conference on Information Technology Interfaces*, June 23–26, pp. 31–40, Cavtat, Croatia.

Widder, A., R.V. Ammon, P. Schaeffer, and C. Wolff. 2007. Identification of Suspicious, Unknown Event Patterns in an Event Cloud. *Proceedings of the 2007 Inaugural International Conference on Distributed Event-Based Systems*, pp. 164–170. Toronto, ON, Canada: ACM.

Widjaya, I. 2011. "Cloud Business 101, Three Types of Cloud Lock-in," *Cloud Business Review.* http://www.cbrdigital.com/2011/05/11/three-types-of-cloud-lock-in.html

Xiao, Z., and Y. Xiao. 2012. "Security and Privacy in Cloud Computing." *IEEE Communications Surveys & Tutorials* 15, no. 2, pp. 843–59.

Yazar, Z. 2002. "A Qualitative Risk Analysis and Management Tool—CRAMM," Version 1.3, *SANS Institute.* https://www.sans.org/reading-room/whitepapers/auditing/qualitative-risk-analysis-management-toolcramm-83

ABOUT THE AUTHOR

Giulio D'Agostino is a system administrator, entrepreneur and cyber security consultant with more than twenty years' experience in the cloud computing, software as a service, and publishing fields. Previously employed by Google, Apple, Hewlett Packard and Salesforce.com. Giulio has lectured at the Technical University of Denmark – DTU, Griffith College Dublin, Web Summit 2016/2017, worked as Irish Tech News contributor and he is currently working as system administrator for SaaS and cloud-based remote connectivity services company LogMeIn Inc.

INDEX

FORTHCOMING TITLES FROM OUR COMPUTER ENGINEERING FOUNDATIONS, CURRENTS, AND TRAJECTORIES COLLECTION

Lisa McLean, *Editor*

- *Data Security in Cloud Computing, Volume II* by Giulio D'Agostino
- *Advanced Selenium Web Accessibility Testing: Software Automation Testing Secrets Revealed* by Narayanan Palani

Momentum Press is one of the leading book publishers in the field of engineering, mathematics, health, and applied sciences. Momentum Press offers over 30 collections, including Aerospace, Biomedical, Civil, Environmental, Nanomaterials, Geotechnical, and many others.

Momentum Press is actively seeking collection editors as well as authors. For more information about becoming an MP author or collection editor, please visit http://www.momentumpress.net/contact

Announcing Digital Content Crafted by Librarians

Concise e-books business students need for classroom and research

Momentum Press offers digital content as authoritative treatments of advanced engineering topics by leaders in their field. Hosted on ebrary, MP provides practitioners, researchers, faculty, and students in engineering, science, and industry with innovative electronic content in sensors and controls engineering, advanced energy engineering, manufacturing, and materials science.

Momentum Press offers library-friendly terms:
- *perpetual access for a one-time fee*
- *no subscriptions or access fees required*
- *unlimited concurrent usage permitted*
- *downloadable PDFs provided*
- *free MARC records included*
- *free trials*

The **Momentum Press** digital library is very affordable, with no obligation to buy in future years.

For more information, please visit **www.momentumpress.net/library** or to set up a trial in the US, please contact **mpsales@globalepress.com**.

CPSIA information can be obtained
at www.ICGtesting.com
Printed in the USA
LVHW020958170720
660950LV00008B/146